The Mortality Merchants

The Mortality Merchants

by G. Scott Reynolds

DAVID McKAY COMPANY, INC.

New York

THE MORTALITY MERCHANTS

FOURTH PRINTING, AUGUST 1969

LIBRARY OF CONGRESS CATALOG CARD NUMBER: 68–19022
MANUFACTURED IN THE UNITED STATES OF AMERICA

This book is dedicated to you, the policyholder, and to your family.

Preface

This book will make full disclosure of precisely what life insurance is, what it can and cannot do, how the basic function of the industry has been all but forgotten, and inform the reader what he can do to acquire the unencumbered death protection that is a necessity for those dependent upon him.

This is not what the industry refers to as a "buy-term-and-invest-the-difference" book. The following pages will not concern themselves with savings, college funds, investments, tax matters, retirement, or any of the other fields of family finance into which life insurance men so insistently meddle—other than to document the industry's own misleading, if not fraudulent, excursions into these areas.

The enormous and needless complexities of life insurance exist for a single purpose—to keep the buyer off balance and in a state of confusion. The inadequacy of regulation of the industry at the state level, and the almost total absence of it at the Federal level, leave the public to fend for itself against the monumental abuses of life insurance.

The purpose of this book is to supply the individual with the knowledge to do this successfully.

Acknowledgment

I would like to express my gratitude to Richard Hardwick for the many months spent assisting editorially in the writing of this book.

Table of Contents

The Mortality Merchants

Introduction

On an overcast afternoon late last February, a 27-year-old real estate salesman was laid to his final rest in a cemetery outside Baltimore, Maryland. As the graveside services came to a close, and the young widow and her two children walked slowly down the hillside toward the parked automobiles, a friend was heard to remark: "I hope Ed had enough life insurance. They're going to need it."

On the same day, across the country in Seattle, Washington, a 27-year-old aircraft design engineer, the victim of a highway crash, was being lowered into his grave. As the funeral procession drove away, one of the pallbearers said to a companion: "Do you suppose he had much life insurance? It's going to be rough on Mary and the kids if he didn't."

Both men, fortunately, did own life insurance. In due time the young widow in Baltimore received a check from a life insurance company whose name and motto are virtual household words. The check was in the amount of $20,000.

In Seattle the engineer's widow also received a check from an equally well-known company. The amount was $105,000.

Both the real estate broker and the engineer had taken out their insurance within a month of each other, and both had paid an annual premium of approximately the same amount. What was the difference that resulted in one family receiving a death payment of more than five times that received by the other? Why, with everything else being equal, will one family face the future with sufficient financial resources to live a comfortable life, while the other finds itself with entirely inadequate means to replace the earning power that was so abruptly cut off?

The answer is not in the rates each of the insurance companies charged, but *in what each man was sold.*

The young Baltimore real estate man, when he was 25, had realized the necessity of life insurance. He discussed it with his wife, and together they went over the budget and decided they could fit in $350—give or take a few dollars— for annual premiums on life insurance. He then talked to a lodge brother who was in the business, and determined he was not going to be "sold," made it very clear that he had a definite sum to allot toward premiums, and that he wanted all the insurance he could get for the money.

The salesman was understanding. He took out his rate book, thumbed past the endowments and other fancy plans, did a bit of figuring, and showed the young man that he could take out a $20,000 policy of "straight" or "whole" life insurance, the cheapest form of "permanent" insurance, for an annual premium of $363.80. The real estate broker checked the figures, nodded, and signed the application.

Meanwhile, in Seattle a similar situation had developed with the young engineer. He had also gotten in touch with an agent and had described his position. He had approximately $350 budgeted for life insurance and he wanted all the protection he could get. The agent consulted the rate book. From a section headed "Term Insurance" he jotted figures onto a sheet of paper. He soon came up with an annual premium of $362.44, which, he said, would provide $110,000 of Decreasing Term Insurance to Age 65.

The young engineer was skeptical. He had heard term insurance described as a poor investment. He had read articles which spoke of term as supplying only temporary needs, as being insurance that was "rented" and not "owned." But the agent pointed out that it offered a great deal of death protection at the time such protection was most needed, when his family was young and entirely dependent upon his present and future earning power, and before any change—physical, moral, financial, or mental—might threaten his future insurability or render him uninsurable.

It made sense, even though there was no mention of retirement income, money for the kids' college education, and other such items stressed in life insurance advertisements. He thought it over for a day or two, made up his mind that it *was* good, and put his name on the application.

The real estate broker in Baltimore was told by his friends that he had made a smart move in taking out "permanent" insurance, while the young engineer in Seattle, when it became known he had bought a term policy, was laughed at and called shortsighted, if not stupid.

Yet, when both men met a premature death two years later, the "shortsighted" man had provided an adequate life insurance estate more than five times that of the "smart" man. Like the vast majority of Americans, neither of them understood the intricacies of life insurance. The insurance agent in Baltimore, in selling his client a $20,000 "permanent" policy, had, in fact, sold him a relatively small decreasing-term policy, coupled with a so-called "savings" or "investment" plan. The salesman, incidentally, had made a first-year commission of $309.23, and, with his client woefully underinsured, had left the door open to come back time and time again to add to his client's life insurance program, while at the same time adding handsomely to his own commissions and renewals.

In Seattle, the life insurance man had done something life insurance men rarely do. He had sold his client pure death protection. From the premium of $362.44 he had earned a first-year commission of $144.98, or considerably less than half the commission paid on the "permanent" policy. He had also eliminated any chance of selling the same client more insurance in the near future, possibly forever.

The practice in life insurance of tying insurance to all sorts of "savings," "investments," retirement plans, college funds, and endless other projects that call for an accumulation of cash, is unique in the insurance industry. Policyholders do not couple a savings plan to their automobile insurance. A home-owner would certainly balk at the suggestion that he reduce the fire insurance on his home from, say, $20,000 to $4,000 so that some of his premium money could be set aside in a "savings" account.

The young man in Baltimore, in buying a $20,000 "perma-nent" policy, had been sold the policy that was best for the agent and the insurance company, not that which was best for his family if he should die or become uninsurable.

The aircraft engineer in Seattle, on the other hand, in his rare good fortune of finding the right agent, had bought a contract that gave the agent and company a fair profit (if it had not, you can be certain the company would not have of-fered it for sale), and at the same time had given the policy-holder what he needed—adequate provision for his family in the event of his death.

Life insurance efficiently does one thing and one thing only. It provides for the future economic value of a man's life in the event the man does not live to provide it himself. Life in-surance should not be bought as if you were going to live 30, 40, 50, or more years; it should be bought as if you were going to die or become uninsurable tomorrow, or even today.

The life insurance industry in the United States, for its own reasons, has from its early origins de-emphasized the actual purpose for its existence by discouraging the sale of pure death protection. The cases just given shed some light on the reasons for this concealment, for if one company could afford to pay a claim of $105,000 while the other paid only $20,000—and the actuarial calculations showed that each could be paid out on policies calling for the same annual premium—then there is the matter of an $85,000 discrepancy somewhere. That discrepancy, multiplied by millions of cases over the past century, accounts for the almost unbelievable accumulation of money that is in the hands of the life in-surance industry.

Chapter 1

Cash Surrender Value—
The Root of the Evil

"On no subject has ignorance so generally prevailed as in life insurance."—Burton J. Hendrick, *The Story of Life Insurance*

Deductible insurance is owned and understood by virtually everyone who has an automobile. A policy containing a $50 deductible clause means simply that the policyholder assumes the financial risk of the first $50 of damage that might be incurred. He is self-insured to this extent; consequently, the premium he pays for his insurance coverage is less than it would be if the company were "on the risk" for the entire claim.

Deductibility is common in many types of insurance. The concept is sound, economical, and very little confusion exists in its use. There is one area in the vast spectrum of insurance, however, in which the word "deductible" is never mentioned, and that is in life insurance.

The word appears nowhere in any life insurance policy. It is never mentioned by the salesmen, or in the companies' folksy advertisements, and in the industry's immaculately planned terminology it has been named *Cash Surrender Value*. More technically, it is called *Level-Premium, Legal Reserve* life insurance; less technically, "permanent" insurance.

Billions of dollars of permanent-type life insurance are sold annually, all under the guise of being a combination of life insurance and a "savings" or "investment" feature. It purports to maintain a level face amount of insurance upon continued payment of a level premium.

In actuality, it is a plan whereby the life insurance company

5

comes off the risk more and more as the years pass, transferring that risk to the owner of the policy. Few policyholders are aware of what is taking place.

Here, in a simple example, is how this legerdemain is performed. A young man takes out $10,000 in straight, or whole, life insurance (the most common form of so-called "permanent" insurance). After a number of years have passed, the policy reaches the point of having, say, a Cash Surrender Value of $3,000. The policyholder interprets this (with careful industry prodding) as meaning he has a "savings account" of $3,000 with the life insurance company. He arrives at this interpretation because this is what the man who sold him the policy told him, and because the constant advertising bombardment of the industry says it is so.

There is a catch, however. What he has *not* been told, and what he does *not* realize, is that he no longer has a $10,000 policy. The face amount of the policy, of course, remains at $10,000. But let's take a close look at precisely what this $10,000 face amount now represents. The $3,000 "savings account" is part of it. The remainder—$7,000—is the amount of life insurance (death protection) he now has.

Should the policyholder die at this point, the company, faithful to its contract, will pay his beneficiaries the face amount of $10,000. It will come in the form of a single check, and there will be no mention that the "savings account" is a substantial part of the total amount. On the contrary; the company will reflect in its statement for the year that a $10,000 death benefit was paid, not a $7,000 death benefit coupled with the return of a $3,000 Cash Surrender Value "savings account."

If the policyholder assumes that the company is actually insuring him continuously for the face amount of the policy—$10,000—then at the time of his death the $3,000 "savings account" is simply being forfeited to the company.

On the other hand, if the company is "on the risk" at the

time of his death for $7,000, then to make up the face amount of $10,000 the policyholder kicks in with the remainder of $3,000. He has, then, paid $3,000 of his own death claim, just as he would have paid $50 toward the repair of a smashed fender under his deductible auto insurance.

There is a basic and important difference in the two, however. Though the deductible figure remains fixed in the case of automobile insurance, it steadily *increases* in the case of the far more essential life insurance.

In all "permanent" or "savings" type life insurance policies, statistics show that the Cash Surrender Value, at age 65, is approximately 50 percent of the face amount of the policy. In other words, a $10,000 policy, when its owner reaches the age of 65, will have a Cash Surrender Value of roughly $5,000. This means, very simply, that the policyholder at that time has a $5,000 deductible life insurance policy. Not only does he have this $5,000, or 50 percent, deductible policy; *the odds are extremely high that he is totally unaware of it.*

The following chart illustrates how this takes place. Column No. 2, bordered in black, is the column that does *not* appear on any of the more than 190 million individual "permanent"-type life insurance policies in force in the United States today. Why is it omitted? Simply because its inclusion would reveal the scheme to the owner of the policy, and would cut disastrously into the sale of "permanent" life insurance.

Solely for the purpose of illustrating the principle involved, the chart is not a replica of the Cash Surrender Value table of an actual policy (though this will be shown later). The formula is simple: at any given year, the total of Column No. 1 and Column No. 2 equals Column No. 3, which is the face amount of the policy. Thus, as the Cash Surrender Value increases (this is your so-called "savings" or "investment"), the amount "at risk" on the part of the company decreases by the same amount. Should the policyholder live to the ultimate maturity of the policy (in "whole" or "straight" life policies

this is now age 100; on policies issued prior to 1948 it is age
96), it can be seen by the last line of the chart that the Cash
Surrender Value (Column 1) has risen to equal the face
amount of the policy, while the amount at risk on the part

Table No. 1

1 Cash Surrender Value (the hidden, increasing deductible)	2 Death Protection, or amount company remains "on the risk"	3 Face Amount of Policy
$ .00	$1,000	$1,000
100	900	1,000
200	800	1,000
300	700	1,000
400	600	1,000
500	500	1,000
600	400	1,000
700	300	1,000
800	200	1,000
900	100	1,000
1,000	0	

of the company (Column 2) has dropped to zero. As insurance companies are inclined to put it, the man has outlived
his insurance.

The truth is that he has done nothing of the sort. He has
simply lived long enough to allow the company to come totally
"off the risk," and is now 100 percent self-insured. The same
principle comes into effect earlier with various types of endowment policies. With endowment at age 65, for example,
the firm is completely "off the risk" at age 65.

When, then, is a $1,000 (or any multiple thereof) life insurance policy *not* a $1,000 life insurance policy? A glance at Table No. 1 will answer the question: when the policy has *any* Cash Surrender Value.

Life insurance came into being so that an individual might share the financial risk of meeting an early or premature death with thousands of other people. It should not exist so that, as Column No. 1 shows, the policyholder might steadily assume part or all of his individual risk. With "permanent" life insurance, as the policy becomes older and the policyholder inevitably moves closer to death, the life insurance company gets increasingly *out* of the life insurance business, while the policyholder gets progressively further into it. This circumstance explains, more than anything else, the reason for the many so-called misunderstandings concerning life insurance.

Americans, from nuclear physicists to ditchdiggers, innocently assume they have their life insurance protection *and* their so-called "savings," or Cash Surrender Value, as well. Nothing could be further removed from the truth and, although it would only take a minute or two for the agent to point this out (if, in fact, he was aware of it himself), life insurance men shy away from it.

It is clearly understood within the industry, however. Bear in mind that the following statement was not made by a critic of the industry and its practices, but by a man from deep within the structure of American life insurance. Dr. S. S. Huebner, who has been described as being the best-known individual in the history of life insurance, in writing of permanent life insurance stated that a life insurance policy is: *"a combination of decreasing term insurance with an accumulating investment. . . ."* [1]

With all its endless names and plans and gimmicks, life insurance has in reality only a single ware to peddle, and that is "term" insurance. Most companies refrain from selling it in its pure form, and the majority of those who will, sell it only as a last resort.

Attention is forcibly focused on the policyholder's paying a level premium throughout the span of the contract, and away from the fact that for this level premium he is being provided less and less protection as time passes. Permanent life insurance, or the so-called "level-premium" plan, was explained by retired actuary, Joseph B. Maclean, as follows:

> . . . under the level premium plan a policy of $1,000 does not give actual insurance of $1,000, but only of $1,000 less the policyholder's own accumulated *excess payments*. . . . *Failure to grasp this simple fact has led to a great deal of misunderstanding of the level-premium plan.*[2] [Emphasis added.]

Again, this is not the writing of a life insurance critic. Mr. Maclean rose, during a long and active career, to the vice presidency of the Mutual Life Insurance Company of New York.

Can these "excess payments" called "Cash Surrender Value," then, be considered a "savings" or "investment" in the true sense of the words?

A pair of life insurance textbook authors—one of whom is presently a paid life insurance lobbyist in the state of Indiana —made the flat statement that "Actuaries would rise up in horror at the suggestion that any part of the premium actually represents pure investment; nevertheless, it is a convenient concept." [3]

There is a disquieting overtone to the words "convenient concept." To whom is this investment concept convenient? Is it to the policyholder, who never discovers he is being led into paying his own death claim with his "excess payments" which have been misleadingly labeled "investment," "savings," "college," "retirement funds"—everything but exactly what they are and were designed to be—part or all of his death claim?

Is it convenient to the widow or other beneficiary who does

not recognize it when it comes back, not as an investment at all, but as an integral part of the death claim check?

The convenience is entirely on the side of the life insurance companies, and the enormity of it literally staggers the mind. According to the *Life Insurance Fact Book,* there was in force in the United States at the beginning of 1966 approximately $428 billion of individual, face-amount life insurance that was nothing more than forms of the hidden and increasing deductible we have described. Of this $428 billion, some 30 percent, or $128 billion, represented the Cash Surrender Values on the more than 190 million separate policies involved.[4] If you owned life insurance at that time which had Cash Surrender Value, you are included in this total, which represents *the amount of risk that the companies had shifted to the policyholders, and without the policyholders knowing it.*

Another of the industry's words for Cash Surrender Value is the "reserve" of a policy. When a policyholder dies, Mr. Maclean went on to write,

> the reserve in respect to his policy makes up part of the amount payable. Thus, the actual "insurance," or "risk," is constantly being reduced. . . . This principle of a reducing amount at risk with correspondingly decreasing "insurance" is fundamental to the level premium system.[5]

The level-premium plan, then, does only one thing. It assures that the policyholder will continue to pay the same premium year after year, and for this unchanging premium he will get less and less death protection, or pure life insurance. The fundamental principle of this type of life insurance is that a $1,000 (or any multiple thereof) life insurance policy does *not* provide $1,000 of life insurance.

A life insurance man, Dr. J. Owen Stalson, writes that the reserve policy provides a constantly decreasing amount of actual protection for which a non-changing rate is charged. *The policyholder usually overlooks this aspect of his insurance situation.*[6] [Emphasis added.]

The men who have been quoted, keep in mind, are *not* critics attacking the century-and-a-quarter-old abuses of the American life insurance industry; rather they are men who have made their livelihoods and their careers within the embrace of this same industry. When they speak and write, they do so among themselves. The quotations make it clear that they are fully aware of the misrepresentations of life insurance, and they are equally aware that the general public is unlikely to overhear them.

Why do so many otherwise intelligent Americans, when confronted with the need for life insurance, find a simple fact impossible to grasp? Why do they overlook the most important aspect of their insurance situation? Why do they have some vague notion that they must buy two separate and distinct things—insurance and an "investment" or "savings" plan— from a life insurance salesman?

How is it that when two men in almost identical circumstances, and who pay identical life insurance premiums, die, one man leaves a life insurance estate more than five times as great as that of the other?

There are a number of answers to these questions. The first is money. Life insurance companies and their agents realize a far greater profit from the sale of the varied forms of "permanent" insurance than they do from the sale of pure death protection. Therefore, it is to their advantage to concentrate their efforts in this area.

The Life Insurance Agency Management Association (LIAMA), which for half a century has been the educational cooperative of the industry and is subsidized by more than 500 life insurance companies, disseminates a great deal of propaganda from the industry point of view which glosses over many important facts inherent in this type of insurance. As an example, in 1961 LIAMA published a book written by Griffin M. Lovelace in which the author stated that an "ordinary, or straight life policy written at the same age [25], and *after providing $100,000 of protection for 40 years,* would have a cash value of about $60,000 at age 65." [7] (Emphasis added.)

The statement is simple and to the point. It is also not completely accurate. But it is, unfortunately, typical of the way the life insurance industry goes about assuring the public that it can have its cake and eat it, too.

Let's take a close look at the situation. As we have seen, the protection under "permanent"-type life insurance declines steadily. Actually, except for the two or three years before any Cash Surrender Value appeared, the policyholder in this example never had $100,000 of protection. If, after 40 years, the Cash Surrender Value (life insurance men have an annoying habit of leaving out the key word—*surrender*—which, by law, must be in the policy) has become approximately $60,000, the protection supplied by the company has dropped to $40,000, or the difference between the face amount and the Cash Surrender Value.

Under the level-premium plan, however, the policyholder is still paying the same premium he began paying 40 years ago, and for which he is now receiving less than half the protection for his premium dollars.

Mr. Lovelace's logic is, to say the least, cloudy. Would he perhaps, for example, say that a man who had been socking away money inside his mattress for 40 years, and who had managed to accumulate $60,000 in this manner, was being provided $60,000 protection by his mattress?

The obsession of life insurance men is with the *premium,* and not with the *actual protection* the company provides, and which melts away at a steady pace.

Further in his book, Lovelace writes, regarding the level-premium plan, that

> it is called level because, although the death rate and cost of insurance increase annually, the level premium is a fixed amount, the same every year. If it is, say, $15 or $20 per $1,000 when a policy is issued to a young man, and he lives and keeps it in force until he is very old, he will still be paying only $15 or $20 per $1,000.[8]

He is certainly correct when he says the death rate and cost of insurance increase annually. Then he performs a miracle on a par with the parting of the Red Sea and tells us that in the case of level-premium life insurance the cost to the policyholder remains the same from youth to very old age. The premium itself *does* remain level, but the premium is the only thing involved that stays the same. The true cost of the protection rises each year, simply because the amount of protection declines each year.

To demonstrate this, let's break Lovelace's $100,000 policy down into 10-year intervals. Based on his statement that the policy will have a Cash Surrender Value of $60,000 after 40 years, we can assume there has been an average increase in Cash Surrender Value of $1,500 per year, or $15,000 every 10 years. He mentions a premium of $15 or $20 per $1,000. Let's split the difference and say that the premium is $17.50 per $1,000, or $1,750 annually for the $100,000 policy. This figure of $1,750 will remain constant throughout the years. It is the level premium.

The following table, broken down into 10-year intervals, shows that while the premium itself remains level, the cost per $1,000 of protection does nothing of the sort.

The figures in Column 3 show the actual "out-of-pocket" cost to the policyholder. This is far from being the true cost. Mr. Lovelace has chosen to ignore entirely the factor of interest. There is, at the end of 40 years, $60,000 in Cash Sur-

Table No. 2

Age	1 Cash Surrender Value (am't. policyholder is self-insured)	2 Amount Company Remains on the Risk (or actual protection)	3 Cost Per $1,000 of Protection
25	$ 0	$100,000	$17.50
35	15,000	85,000	20.59
45	30,000	70,000	25.00
55	45,000	55,000	31.82
65	60,000	40,000	43.75

render Value. This, at the modest return of 4 percent, will earn $2,400 in interest in a single year. (Chapter 2 will cover this detail, but it is of such magnitude that it should be touched upon here.)

What happens to the interest being earned on the $60,000? It does *not* come to the policyholder, even though this Cash Surrender Value is the "savings" or "investment" for which he bought this particular policy 40 years earlier. He is, then, giving up the interest on his money to the life insurance company. Therefore, the lost interest should be figured into the cost of his declining protection.

His total cost—$1,750 in his annual level premium, plus $2,400 in lost interest (4 percent simple interest on $60,000 for one year)—is $4,150 during the fortieth year. Meanwhile, the actual protection—or the amount the company remains "on the risk"—has plummeted to $40,000. A bit of arithmetic (the number of $1,000s—40—divided into the total cost, $4,150) shows that the true cost per $1,000 of protection is now $103.75, or approximately 500 percent higher than Lovelace's $15 or $20 per $1,000.

The example of a $100,000 "permanent" policy having a $60,000 Cash Surrender Value at age 65 is relatively typical of the ratio for all such policies. Northwestern Mutual Life

Insurance Company, for example, paid out roughly $100 million (to be exact, $101,972,073.14) in what the company's 1964 annual report described as "death benefits." However, $60,605,343 of this was the deceased policyholders' Cash Surrender Value "savings" coming back to the beneficiaries as part of the death claims.

In other words, Northwestern Mutual had come "off the risk" for 60 percent of the total, and the policyholders who died that year had passed on with more than $60 million of *deductible* life insurance.

Another life insurance man, Dr. Joseph M. Belth, approached the cost of life insurance from a different tack, one that touched on fundamental changes that true price disclosure might bring about. Belth warned that "widespread price disclosure could conceivably undermine the concept of level-premium life insurance." [9] If such a reasonable thing as revealing the actual cost of a basic necessity such as life insurance could undermine the concept, then it appears obvious that there is something basically faulty about the concept.

The fundamental fact to remember is that "level-premium" life insurance is not level-*cost* life insurance. The concept will be undermined when a sufficient number of people come to realize that "level-premium" is nothing more than a hyphenated pair of words used to relieve *them* of *their* money under false pretenses.

There is, very simply, no such thing as level-premium life insurance.

Chapter 2

Cash Surrender Value and Foregone Interest

"In the calculation of the yearly prices per $1,000 of protection, this steady increase stems from the combined effect of two factors —the increasing amount of foregone interest and the declining amount of protection as the savings element grows larger."
—Dr. Joseph M. Belth, CLU, CPCU,
The Retail Price Structure in American Life Insurance

"Through what other medium can you start, with the payment of the first premium, a compound interest savings account that is riskless, that guarantees the interest credited will not fall below a contractual floor, that sets no ceiling as to what may be earned?"

According to President O. Kelly Anderson, of New England Life,[1] who posed the question, the only medium capable of this is permanent-type, Cash Surrender Value life insurance.

The interest supposedly being earned by policyholders on their Cash Surrender Value "savings accounts" (in most cases the New York State Department of Insurance does not permit insurance companies to represent Cash Surrender Values as savings accounts) is one of the most productive gimmicks the industry has come up with. It is also a widespread misconception which the industry has not seen fit to dispel—perhaps because it is extremely helpful in the sale of "permanent"-type life insurance.

Even after an individual understands the true nature of Cash Surrender Value—that it does nothing more than let the company come "off the risk" with his money—he is likely to rationalize this with something like: "Well, that may be so, but I get a guaranteed tax-free interest rate on my Cash Surrender Value."

Whether the annual addition to the Cash Surrender Value of a policy comes from interest earned or, as actuary Joseph B. Maclean claimed, from "excess premiums," or a mixture of both, is of no importance. What is important is that it does not come to the policyholder, but is simply imputed to the Cash Surrender Value of the policy. This fact in itself refutes the theory that the owner of the policy receives any interest, for his "savings account"—principal *and* interest—comes to his beneficiary as a part of the death claim check that makes up the face value of the policy. During the lifetime of the policyholder, all of the Cash Surrender Value, principal *and* interest, is lumped together and becomes the amount at any given time in which the company has come "off the risk."

The truth of interest earned on Cash Surrender Values was stated very plainly by actuary Maclean when he wrote:

> A good deal of misunderstanding in connection with . . . the annual cost of an insurance policy is the annual premium paid. It is evident that part of this cost where the policy has a cash surrender value is represented by interest on that cash value. . . . The company actually holds the amount of the cash value, and earns interest upon it *which is not paid to the policyholder. The insured therefore pays over the interest on his cash value just as clearly as if he held the cash value himself, earned the interest upon it, and paid the interest to the company.*[2] [Emphasis added.]

Maclean's statement is easily proven by anyone owning a life insurance policy that has any Cash Surrender Value. All he has to do is borrow his Cash Surrender Value from the company. As long as the policyholder has this loan of his own money, he will have to pay interest to the company. This should make it crystal-clear who is receiving the interest on Cash Surrender Values.

The interest that policyholders are giving over to the life insurance companies is no small amount. At the beginning of 1966 the 1,700-odd life companies operating in the United States held more than $128 *billion* in Cash Surrender Values. At the rate of 4 percent (which any policyholder could earn by depositing his money in a savings bank), the interest policyholders unwittingly gave up in a single year would come to more than *five billion dollars.*

When a company admits to this interest being lost by its policyholders (and this is rare), it is done in a manner that makes it appear of little or no consequence. In a booklet entitled *The A B C of Life Insurance,* published in a kindergarten format by Mutual Life Insurance Company of New York (MONY) with the declared purpose of explaining "what life insurance is," the case of a 35-year-old man taking out $10,000 of "straight" or "whole" life is used in an attempt to prove that "permanent" insurance is a bargain unequaled anywhere in the field of finance. Just beneath a chart that endeavors to convince the reader that after carrying the policy for 30 years, the then 65-year-old policyholder finds his insurance has cost him nothing, there is this statement:

". . . except for the loss of interest on his money during the period he was insured."

The lack of understanding of Cash Surrender Value interest earnings has ensnared tens of millions of policyholders who accept the advice of life insurance salesmen. But in 1964 the net came up with a most unexpected fish—the American Bar Association, which should have known better. The subject arose when a tax reform committee of the ABA suggested to the Internal Revenue Service that it was overlooking a tremendous untapped source of income in allowing the interest earned *by life insurance policyholders* on "their" Cash Surrender Values to get by "income tax free."

The Life Insurance Association of America (LIAA), whose membership is comprised of more than a hundred of the country's giant companies, immediately thrust its president and general counsel, Mr. Eugene Maurice Thoré, into the breach. Thoré, who is recognized as one of the top legal minds in the industry, made it very clear that the policyholders were not liable for such taxation, and for the simplest of reasons: they were not *receiving* the interest on their so-called "savings accounts." In straightening out both the IRS and his fellow lawyers, Thoré said:

> The owner of a level premium life insurance policy does not receive a current economic benefit as the policy reserve [Author's note: Cash Surrender Value] in the hands of the company earns interest. The policy provisions make this abundantly clear. There is no provision in the policy which says he owns a part of the company reserve. [Author's note: Whatever happened to that "compound-interest savings account"?] There is no provision which says that interest is being earned for him on any part of the company reserve. To the contrary, the principal policy terms describe promises to pay benefits in certain events—usually upon death or upon living to a certain date or age.
>
> The right to cash value upon surrender of the policy or the right to borrow against the cash value are, however, sometimes viewed as suggesting the ownership of a fund in the hands of the company upon which interest is being earned. Perhaps this misconception forms the basis of the conclusion that the policyholder is enjoying current interest income that should be taxed.
>
> *It is true that in our sales talks and to some extent in our actuarial reasoning we have attributed to the cash value of a life insurance policy some of the characteristics of a savings*

account. But this popular notion is without legal foundation.[3]
[Emphasis added.]

Thoré, in admitting that life insurance sales talks attribute
the "characteristics" of a savings account to Cash Surrender
Values, while at the same time stating flatly that the "popular
notion is without legal foundation," leads the owner of such
insurance to a most interesting question. If the product—
permanent-type life insurance—is such a wonderful investment
for the policyholder and his family, why are all sorts of subter-
fuge necessary in order to sell it?

The LIAA, incidentally, did not respond with such force
to the American Bar Association's suggestion in order to keep
the masses of policyholders from paying taxes. It was protecting the industry's fair-haired, money-making child—permanent-type life insurance.

Let's examine a specific policy to see what an insured person really obtains for the premiums he pays. The following
table was taken from a policy once owned by the author. The
particular policy was what is referred to as a "graded-premium"
or "modified life" policy, which means that the annual premium started low, increased during each of the first five
years, and then leveled off. The low starting premiums put off
the appearance of any Cash Surrender Value until the end of
the fourth year.

With the exception of the center column showing the yearly
increase in Cash Surrender Value per $1,000 of the face
amount, the table is just as it appeared on the policy.

The added column showing the annual *increase* in Cash
Surrender Value illustrated clearly that, after the initial
appearance of Cash Surrender Value ($8 after the fourth
year), the annual addition leveled off, with only a slight
variation, up and down, of a dollar or two.

If, as most life insurance salesmen would have you believe,
such Cash Surrender Value is a compound-interest "savings

Table No. 3

At End of Policy Year	Actual Yearly Increase in Cash Surrender Value (*This column never shown in policy*)		Cash Surrender Value For Each $1,000 of the Sum Insured
1			None
2			None
3			None
4	plus $ 8	equals	$ 8
5	" 16	"	24
6	" 17	"	41
7	" 17	"	58
8	" 17	"	75
9	" 18	"	93
10	" 18	"	111
11	" 18	"	129
12	" 19	"	148
13	" 18	"	166
14	" 19	"	185
15	" 19	"	204
16	" 17	"	221
17	" 18	"	239
18	" 17	"	256
19	" 18	"	274
20	" 17	"	291

Age			
55	$18 per year—7 years equals		417
60	18 *per year—5 years equals		506
65	17 *per year—5 years equals		592

* By interpolation and rounding of figures, amounts do not work out exactly.

account," why isn't each annual addition larger than the preceding year's? At the end of the twentieth year (and every year after that) the original $8 representing the first Cash Surrender Value remains just that—$8. Where is the 20 years of compound interest that has been earned on this money? It is in the hands of the company, exactly where it has always been.

The Cash Surrender Value table contained in the policy did not show the additions beyond age 65, or to age 100, at which time such "whole" or "straight" life insurance policies endow. Another curiosity comes to light when these figures are worked out.

The face amount of the policy being $10,000, according to the table the Cash Surrender Value would have been 10 times $592, or $5,920 at age 65. This means that the company would be "on the risk" for the difference between the face amount ($10,000) and the Cash Surrender Value, or $4,080. When the policy endowed at age 100, the CSV would equal the face amount of the policy. This means that there are 35 years remaining in which the "on the risk" of the company would decline to zero. By dividing the 35 years into the $4,080, we find that during these later years the average annual increase in the Cash Surrender Value is $11.66 per $1,000, considerably less than during the earlier years.

The premium is being paid each year, the death protection is steadily dropping, and yet the annual addition in Cash Surrender Value declines. If this is compound interest, it appears to be working in reverse.

This is what is sometimes referred to as "foregone" interest.

While compound interest is withheld from the policyholder, it has worked miracles for the industry. The Mutual Benefit Life Insurance Company, for example, made its first investment of premium dollars shortly after issuing its first policy in 1844. In the century-plus since then the interest income of the company has exceeded $800 million, a sum sufficient to pay all expenses and taxes since the organization of the company and still leave more than $380 million on the company books.

Thus the life insurance industry has created two extremely misleading concepts which the public has swallowed in their entirety—(1) that Cash Surrender Values are synonymous with "savings accounts," and (2) that the owner of Cash Surrender Value-type life insurance earns compound interest on this fictitious "savings account" while it is in the possession of the company. Both concepts combine to deceive the policyholder as to the true price he pays for his life insurance, and it is full-price disclosure that the industry fears. Dr. Joseph N. Belth wrote:

> In the calculation of the yearly prices per $1,000 of protection, this steady increase [in the yearly price] stems from the combined effect of two factors—the increasing amount of foregone interest and the declining amount of protection as the savings element grows larger. In other words, neither the leveling of premiums nor the contracting of premiums into a limited period of years (such as in a twenty-payment life policy) levels out the yearly prices per $1,000 of protection. Rather, the leveling of premiums merely modifies the premium outlay pattern from what it would be on a yearly renewable term policy. Many of the misunderstandings surrounding cash value life insurance—and, indeed, much of the mystery that surrounds the operation of life insurance companies—may stem from a general unawareness on the part of the buying public concerning these basic characteristics of level-premium life insurance.[4]

Dr. Belth suggests that full disclosure of the prices of life insurance be spread over a period of 20 years to avoid the disruptive effect it might possibly have if done too abruptly. From the point of view of the industry this might be desirable. However, it should be remembered that the abuses have been going unchecked for more than a hundred years, and during that time the industry has done nothing to disclose to the public the true cost of death protection.

From the point of view of the present owner of "permanent" types of life insurance, and the man contemplating its purchase, full disclosure is essential today, for the simple reason there is something he, as an individual, can do about it. Unlike the price of drugs, electricity, gas, or thousands of other necessities and near-necessities in the modern world, the cost of life insurance can be examined by the individual and, once understood, he can buy it in the form of pure death protection. With an understanding of the nature of Cash Surrender Value, and an awareness of the vast sums of money foregone in interest, the individual does not have to wait for the government to come to his aid. He can do something about it himself.

Chapter 3

Cash Surrender Value—
The Phantom Tax Dodge

"The economy of the life insurance company as an efficient
mechanism for the gathering of a tax from a large group is
little discussed."
—Dr. J. Owen Stalson, *Marketing Life Insurance*

Seldom is heard even a whispered word about the taxes
that life insurance policyholders actually pay. A great deal of
shouting, however, is heard about what the industry calls
"the favorable tax status that life insurance enjoys." So much
emphasis has been placed on this as a sales device that it often
appears that this "tax status" is the primary purpose of life
insurance.

Tax-Free Interest

Interest earned on Cash Surrender Values, you have probably been told, is *tax-free* to the policyholder. This has an appealing ring to a tax-conscious prospective buyer, and it is
true. The thing that has been omitted, however, is the basic
reason the policyholder pays no tax on such interest. That
reason was shown in the previous chapter, when the American Bar Association suggested to the Internal Revenue Service that it should begin collecting taxes on this interest. The
life insurance industry itself then made it abundantly clear
that it would be highly irregular to tax policyholders for income they were *not* receiving.

26

Premium and Other Taxes

Policyholders *do* pay taxes, and the life companies are themselves the tax collectors. Approximately $5.40 of each $100 of all premiums paid to life insurance companies is earmarked for taxes.[1] The ultimate source of all money in the hands of the companies is the premium-paying customer, and taxes—just like sales commissions and the scores of other expenses of the company—are actuarially calculated into the premium.

As an example of the scope of the hidden tax being paid by policyholders, the annual report of Northwestern Mutual Life Insurance Company showed state premium taxes, licenses, fees, and Federal income taxes of $36.5 million, paid for the year 1964. In that same year, as we saw in Chapter 1, the company claimed to have paid death benefits of approximately $100 million. Of this $100 million, more than $60 million was in Cash Surrender Values, or the "savings accounts" of deceased policyholders which came to the beneficiaries as part of the total death claims. Thus, by subtracting $60 million from $100 million, we find the actual "on the risk" death payments made by the company were $40 million. In other words, Northwestern Mutual paid out roughly $3.5 million more in death claims than it paid out in taxes.

Here we have an example of a company which pays out almost as much in taxes as it does in death claims. The payment of death claims is the basic reason for the existence of life insurance companies. The pooling of premium dollars makes this function possible. But what about the $36.5 million paid in one year in taxes? Who paid that? It was not the company, for with the tax burden being calculated as a part of the premiums, the company simply acted as tax collector, passing along the policyholders' money to the proper governmental agencies.

In 1966 Robert E. Slater, president of John Hancock Mutual Life Insurance Company, expressed chagrin at discovering that "few people knew we paid any taxes at all." Mr. Slater may have been thinking of the $66 million that John Hancock collected from its policyholders that year, and which it turned over to the city, state, and Federal governments.

Life insurance executives may feel chagrin at the public's ignorance of these taxes, but few if any would express surprise. The industry soft-pedals any mention of the taxes it (or, more accurately, the policyholder) pays, and for a very basic reason. If the policyholders and prospective policyholders became truly aware of this great tax burden they were being called upon to bear—not just on the death protection of a policy but on their so-called "savings" and "investment" portion as well—the selling process would be severely impeded, and these "savings-investment" funds would be shaken loose from vital death protection and put into other media where no gross taxes, commissions, or other company costs were deducted.

The over-all tax burden is staggering. The life insurance industry provides the largest single source of totally hidden taxes in the United States. Taxes paid to local, state, and Federal governments, plus licenses and fees, totaled $1.4 billion in 1965, and the figure grows yearly. The life companies claim that they are paying this tax bill, but insurance man—author Griffin M. Lovelace got to the heart of the matter: "In the various states annual taxes are levied on the premiums, and they have become a heavy, as well as unjust, burden on the policyholder, a penalty on thrift." [2]

Calling the state premium tax a "penalty on thrift" would seem to indicate the writer was bemoaning the tax being levied on that part of the premium destined for the "savings," or Cash Surrender Value of permanent insurance. Where, then, is the thrift in having a "savings account" which bears no interest while in the hands of the life insurance company,

where all "deposits" are taxed at almost every level of government, and which at the time of the policyholder's death is
confiscated by the company to help pay the death claim?

The Tax Goes Up

Sam Jones has an "ordinary life" policy on which he pays
a level premium from first year to last, whether that be 10,
20, or 50 years in the future. That part of his premium earmarked for taxes (5.4 percent, or $5.40 of each $100 of
premium paid, is the average throughout the country) can be
properly considered the tax he pays in the beginning for
$10,000 of protection. As Jones' Cash Surrender Value begins
to accumulate, however, his actual death protection, or the
amount the company is "on the risk," declines in direct proportion. When his CSV has reached $5,000, then, his death
protection has dropped to $5,000, the sum of the two being
the face amount of the policy. The premium, however, has
remained the same, and so has that portion of the premium
going for taxes. Jones is paying the same tax on $5,000 death
protection that he paid years before on $10,000. Simple arith-
metic shows that he is now paying a 10.8 percent tax where
he was originally paying half that, or 5.4 percent.

This is a strange phenomenon, indeed, when almost a billion and a half dollars in taxes are virtually unheard of by the
people being taxed.

Dr. S. S. Huebner referred to this state of ignorance when
he wrote:

> The present heavy taxation of life insurance is attributable
> chiefly to general ignorance on the part of the public and the
> lawmakers of the true nature of legal reserve life insurance,
> and to the fact that taxes on this business, especially those
> levied on gross premiums, are so easily collected.[3]

Who is to disturb this general ignorance? Government is
not likely to step in without a great deal of prodding, for it

is far simpler to collect a single large tax payment than scores
of millions of smaller ones. Two life insurance companies
alone—the Prudential and Metropolitan—have more than 45
million policyholders *each*. Federal, state, and local governments find it considerably easier to deal with two companies
than with 90 million individuals.

Nor are the companies themselves likely to embark on a
course of public education that is diametrically opposed to
selling practices which have long since proved their tremendous profitability.

Income and Estate "Tax-Frees"

Millions of policyholders have been told by their life insurance salesmen that the proceeds of their policies are "income tax-free" and "estate tax-free."

The first of these is true, but not for the implied reason.
All assets of an estate are income tax-free, as there is no income tax after death.

The latter is true to an extent, and also not for the reason
implied. Since 1948 the Federal Government has allowed the
first $60,000 of an estate to go estate tax-free. (Through
proper legal and accounting guidance, a married couple can
easily double this allowance to $120,000.) The allowance in-
cludes not only life insurance death payments, but all other
assets of the estate as well.

The high cost of permanent Cash Surrender Value life
insurance—$20, $30, $40 and more per $1,000—precludes
the buying of large policies on the part of the average American. A man who is sold a $10,000 "permanent" policy with
an annual premium of several hundred dollars—rather than
five or ten times as much pure death protection for the same
premium—is likely to leave an estate well under the tax-
exempt $60,000. In practice, then, the sale of permanent types
of life insurance often ensures that an estate will not be large

enough to take full advantage of this important exemption. The general belief that life insurance enjoys special handling is extremely widespread. A recent survey revealed that 41 percent of successful individuals interviewed in three widely separated cities believed that life insurance proceeds were not included in the estate for Federal tax purposes.[4] Some few *states* do have this special handling of life insurance, but here again it is very important to have plenty of pure death protection so that full advantage can be taken of the tax laws.

Vast amounts of life insurance are sold to supply a sort of "clean-up fund" upon the death of the insured. Among the items this fund is represented as taking care of is the estate tax. The belief that life insurance bought for this purpose is itself tax-free has become so universal that the Internal Revenue Service has found it necessary to make an explicit statement in the Estate Tax Return (Form 706), which must be filed on estates exceeding $60,000. This may well be the only statement included in any tax form specifically to explain away a misleading sales practice. On page 12 of Form 706 there is the following sentence: "Insurance in favor of an estate includes insurance effected to provide funds to meet the estate tax."

Life insurance men have a wide variety of hats from which to select for any particular occasion. One hat is that of "tax expert," or "estate counselor." In 1964 Lambert M. Huppeler, New England Life Insurance Company's New York general agent, formed an estate planning department. Writing in a trade journal, Huppeler said that the new department actually "was just a proposal department, *but estate planning sounded more impressive.*" [5] (Emphasis added.)

In other words, the estate planning department was nothing more than a gimmick, another of the life insurance practices which, among other things, have at least 41 percent of otherwise intelligent Americans believing that life insurance proceeds are not included in an estate for Federal tax purposes.

This new department, incidentally, Huppeler went on to say with pride, worked out very well for the agency:

> Cases became larger and larger, commissions became higher and higher. . . . Most important, the estate planning department paid for itself in its very first year.

Death and taxes and the inevitability of both go hand in hand, and life insurance men are not above using this tie to increase the sale of their product. The point to keep in mind is that life insurance, regardless of the purpose for which it was bought, is just as taxable in an estate as an automobile, a house, a farm, money in the bank, or any other asset of the estate.

The Tax of Inflation

In January, 1966, President Lyndon Johnson said to the Congress in his Economic Report that inflation "is the most unjust and capricious form of taxation that the American public is called upon to pay." For that large segment of the American public that owns any Cash Surrender Value life insurance, the tax of inflation is not only unjust and capricious; it is also virtually unknown and totally unnecessary.

In the span of only 26 years, from 1940 to 1966, the value of the dollar dropped 57 percent. One dollar in 1966, in other words, would have a purchasing power of only 43 cents, or 57 cents less than the dollar that existed in 1940. As an example of the effect of this on life insurance "savings," let's take a man who owns a $10,000 permanent-type life insurance policy. Let's assume that this policy, in 1940, had a Cash Surrender Value of $1,000. As we saw in the previous chapter, the $1,000 is earning interest for the life insurance company, not for the policyholder; therefore the $1,000 from

1940 will remain $1,000 in 1966. However, it will not buy what it would have in 1940. It has dropped to 43 percent of its original purchasing power. Therefore, by "saving" with his life insurance company the policyholder has allowed his "savings" to dwindle steadily throughout the 26-year span, and the more Cash Surrender Value he had, the more he lost to the tax of inflation.

Historian Arnold Toynbee said he never studied a civilization whose currency didn't eventually peter out. Inflation has been with man from time immemorial, and there is no reason to think it will stop now.

The managers of life insurance companies are in a position to take measures that will lessen the rate of inflation, and consequently preserve some of the purchasing power of money entrusted to them by their policyholders. A high percentage of these men, however, are stockholders, directors, or officers of other enterprises which may conflict with their interest in the welfare of policyholders. A nonprofit, objective organization, the American Institute for Economic Research, had this to say of such men:

> Their other corporate interest and their personal fortunes benefit from inflation. . . . Therefore, we feel that policyholders and prospective policyholders should no longer entrust their accumulated savings to the managers of life insurance companies.[6]

The amount of money lost in this manner by policyholders who have entrusted their money to the managers of life insurance companies, for the 26-year period of 1940–1966, has been figured at more than $55.5 billion.[7] This tremendous loss has come about solely through the industry's insistence on selling permanent-type, Cash Surrender Value, level-premium life insurance. Concerning a possible solution to loss to inflation by life insurance policyholders, Professor Charles R. Whittlesey, of the Wharton School of Finance (which is heavily endowed by life insurance companies), wrote:

> A partial relief for this situation [creeping inflation] would be to reduce greatly the proportion of insurance sold which embodies a substantial savings element. Much greater emphasis would come to be placed on term insurance.[8]

Professor Whittlesey also observed that inflation

> may legitimately be regarded as one of the dangers against which insurance leaders should be constantly alert but it would be bad public policy for the country as a whole and bad public relations for the life insurance industry in particular ever to acknowledge that inflation, creeping or otherwise, is inevitable.[9]

The insurance which embodies a "substantial savings element" is, of course, "permanent" CSV insurance. Not only should a policyholder avoid these life insurance "savings plans" which are actually automatic "losing plans," but from the point of view of life insurance he should hedge against inflation by buying much larger amounts of the much lower-priced forms of "term" insurance. By doing this, he guarantees that his beneficiaries—who will be receiving cheaper dollars—will receive a sufficient amount of them.

Chapter 4

Cash Surrender Value—
History

"I became persuaded that life insurance was the most available, convenient, and permanent breeding place for rogues that civilization had ever presented."
—Elizur Wright, first insurance commissioner of Massachusetts

Typifying the evangelistic view of permanent life insurance and its elusive "savings plan" spread far and wide by the industry was a letter written in 1963 by Mr. A. Jack Nussbaum, president of Northern States Life Insurance Company:

Are we a bunch of sissies? . . . I insist that if we believe that Life Insurance has all the attributes we claim it has, then we should shout from the housetops that we are Life Insurance men, and to "hell" with any other savings media. . . . Everyone agrees that the Ten Commandments are sound. Life Insurance is sound. . . . It is the first and foremost savings plan ever devised by the human mind that will do all the good things that Life Insurance can and will do.[1]

The Ten Commandments we can go along with. But the simple fact is that "level-premium," "permanent-type," Cash Surrender Value life insurance was never devised by the human mind to be a savings plan at all, let alone the "first and foremost." It came about entirely by accident, an unexpected and forced by-product of the level-premium concept. Somewhere along the line life insurance men have found it convenient to lose sight of their industry's beginnings, and in the light of the record it has scrawled across the years, this is understandable.

The idea of a policyholder paying a level premium through-out the contract of his life insurance came into being in the late eighteenth century—the brain child of a group of Englishmen, among whom was Edmund Halley, better remembered for the comet bearing his name. Using the first tables of mortality, they calculated the cost of insuring a life from any given age to the life expectancy at that age, and then, by transferring part of the prohibitively high cost at later ages to the lower costs at younger ages, arrived at a level premium.

The payments (then, as now) in the earlier years of a contract were a great deal higher than the mortality tables indicated they should be, and as a consequence, huge reserves of these overpayments began to accrue. The money accumulated in this manner was considered to be the sole property of the companies.

This remained virtually unchanged during the first half of the nineteenth century in the United States, at the time life insurance began to gain a foothold. The policyholder was contractually assured only of the death claim. There was nothing in the policy about Cash Surrender Values, nothing remotely hinting at a reserve that might be interpreted as a "savings plan." There was no grace period in the payment of premiums, and policies could—and did—become "inoperative," or lapse, for any of a dozen reasons. When this happened, all premiums already paid to the company were forfeited.

This process placed vast fortunes in the hands of the companies. There was none of the missionary-like zeal presently displayed (at least outwardly) by life insurance men wishing to share this wealth with the people who provided it. In fact, the opposite was true. Efforts to broach the subject of non-forfeiture (the return to the policyholder, in some form, of a share of the reserve) were invariably put aside.

Policyholders' losses resulting from the lapsing of policies and the accompanying forfeiture, even in the years before the rapid expansion of the industry, were heavy. In 1859, in Massachusetts alone, life insurance policyholders gave up $234,000 in this manner.

Many companies, through pamphlets, advertisements, and sales practices, began to draw parallels between life insurance and savings banks, which were popular at the time. They were careful, however, to leave such enticements out of the policy itself, and regardless of what the would-be policyholder thought as a result of the sales pitch that won him over, the policy was—and still *is*—the contract. The Mutual Life Insurance Company of New York (MONY), for example, had a sentence in its policy which read: "And it is further agreed, that in every case where this policy shall cease, or become null and void, previous payments made thereon shall be forfeited to said company."

The question naturally arises: why did people buy something which contractually refuted the glowing descriptions of the salesmen? The answer a century ago was probably as simple as it is today. Few, if any, individuals ever read their policies, and those who did quickly became lost in a jungle of verbiage. The policies were so complex and involved that a New Hampshire judge was prompted to write concerning them:

> Seldom has the art of typography been so successfully diverted from the diffusion of knowledge to the suppression of it. There was ground for the premium payer to argue that the print alone was evidence, competent to be submitted to a jury, of a fraudulent plot.[2]

Historically, most real change in life insurance has come from outside the industry. Regulation was virtually nonexistent, just as it is today, and the companies were curbed by nothing more than considerations of public credulity and what the individual situation would bear.

Some companies claimed to have allowed loans against policies and given Cash Surrender Values a century ago, even though no provision for either was in the contract. If true, these were isolated and special cases, and the fact remained that it was *not* specified in the policy, and the policy was the sole binding agreement between policyholder and company.

The insistence by the industry on forfeiture in the case of any lapsed policy led, perhaps inevitably, to a revolt on the part of the policyholders. There were other inequities, but as the public became somewhat aware of the true nature of "level-premium" life insurance, it felt it should have some claim to the vast reserves created by overpayments.

One of the prime movers in the fight to force the life insurance companies to correct this injustice was Elizur Wright, the first Insurance Commissioner of Massachusetts. The three nonforfeiture provisions in modern life insurance are in large measure due to his persistent efforts. In 1861 his labors brought about a state law in Massachusetts requiring life insurance companies to provide extended-term insurance to policyholders who, for one reason or another, were unable or unwilling to continue paying premiums. This provision, in most cases, was still heavily in favor of the companies (as a later chapter on extended-term insurance will explain). However, it was an improvement over the total forfeiture that preceded it.

At least one company, New York Life, foresaw Wright's success in establishing a beachhead in nonforfeiture, and introduced an alternate by allowing paid-up insurance. (This, too, was more favorable to the company than to the policyholder, and will be covered later.)

The industry seemed willing to do almost anything to avoid giving money to policyholders or their beneficiaries. The 1860s were a period when life insurance introduced many novelties which, according to a writer of the time, included almost every form of policy which ingenuity could suggest, and which offered any reasonable expectation of meeting favor, including numberless schemes of transforming one into another at the option of the holder. Almost every new company desired some fresh device for which it might claim the credit of a special feature, and the ingenuity of the experts was taxed.[3]

Yet, even with their willingness to turn life insurance upside down, inside out, or any other way so that it might appear new and different, they continued to stand firmly against any cash nonforfeiture concessions. As the public clamor continued, and the lapsing of policies grew, the industry began to cast about for a new gimmick. The Tontine plan was the apparent answer. The president of Connecticut Mutual Life Insurance Company, Jacob L. Greene, wrote that as

policies were dropping off with fearful rapidity, the refinement of ingenuity appeared in a plan which would make the loss of business itself a basis for new and overwhelming attractions, and yet defer for many years all expectation of a dividend. The Tontine plan was launched; tables exhibited the rapid loss of policies, not as a result of bad work or loss of confidence, but to show how large a sum of money might be realized from that source for the benefit of those who did not drop out; and calculations devised upon this basis were made to show how few out of a Tontine class would probably remain policyholders at the end of ten or fifteen years, and how much those departing would leave behind for the more persistent or more fortunate.[4]

The Equitable Life Assurance Society of the United States initiated the plan in 1867 to save itself, it has been alleged, from threatened bankruptcy. Other companies soon climbed aboard for the ride. The Tontine policy was described in an 1873 sales booklet put out by the Equitable as follows:

The surplus (commonly called the "profits" from which dividends are paid) on such policies is ascertained and declared at the end of ten, fifteen, or twenty years, as may have been elected by the assured at the time of his application. The amount of every policy terminating by death in the interval is paid, but without profits, the latter being accumulated by those who survive. Persons discontinuing their payments before the profits are divided, receive no surrender value for their policies, but forfeit the same, including profits, for the benefit of those who continue.[5]

In other words, the Tontine plan of life insurance was nothing more than a society in which it was to the great financial advantage of each participant that all his fellows fall by the wayside, at the eleventh hour if possible. Massachusetts Commissioner Elizur Wright condemned it as "life insurance cannibalism. It is as if a temperance society should endeavor to promote its cause by establishing a liquor saloon under its lecture room, or a church should support its minister by a lottery." [6]

But the Tontine plan was not all smooth sailing for the companies. By 1880 it was running into trouble. More than 100,000 policies had been dropped, and with no legal recourse against the companies, considerable ill will arose among the thousands who had dropped out. Even those who were able to continue paying premiums throughout the Tontine period were enraged at the way company mismanagement and unaccountable slush funds had eroded the "kitty" they were to share in.

The shadow of nonforfeiture continued to lengthen over the industry. A nonforfeiture law was passed by the New York legislature in 1879. The life companies managed to have an amendment tacked onto the bill specifying that a clause waiving nonforfeiture could be included in the policy, but the vote-conscious legislators ruled that such a clause must appear in red ink, obviously so that the policyholder would stand a fair chance of discovering it amid the foliage. The New York Life Insurance Company immediately *began to print the entire policy in red ink!*

It was difficult, if not totally impossible, for effective regulation and legislation to develop under the conditions that prevailed. The companies wielded far too much power. Their managers were described as being "the darlings of commerce and industry." There were occasional investigations, such as one in 1877 inquiring into the relations between the New York insurance commissioner's office and the life insurance companies operating in the state.

The legislative committee uncovered so much dirt that the Big Three—the Equitable, New York Life, and Mutual of New York—had the record bowdlerized. A political opportunist, William S. Manning, secured a complete copy of the committee record, however, and brought it out in book form. The companies bought up the entire printing, and Manning himself was effectively silenced by an annual retainer for years afterward.[7]

So powerful was the industry that no one seemed beyond its influence. Elizur Wright was himself quieted by a retainer from the Equitable Society until his death in 1885.

Silencing of the press was effective, but not complete. A contemporary journalist observed that "companies were too easily formed and were too often mere hospitals for broken down merchants, incompetent clergymen, or ruined adventurers, whose knowledge of insurance does not qualify them to define the word, and who would serve their generation far better by taking to the country, and there cultivating, at the same time, cabbages and themselves." [8]

With virtually no supervision, the industry continued its reckless journey through the last two decades of the nineteenth century. Thoughts of central control began to crop up, but, just as now, they ran into stiff opposition. One opponent warned: "If the door is once opened, it is opened to federal

supervision of another class of business. . . . What we want
to do is set our faces against the first step." [9]

The *Commercial and Financial Chronicle* reminded its
readers that insurance, being private enterprise, was "a business which offers the least conceivable occasion or excuse for
anything which savors of . . . government control." [10]

The growing clamor of the public could not be forever
denied, however, and in 1905 a committee of the New York
legislature, under the chairmanship of Senator William W.
Armstrong, began an investigation of the Big Three—the
Equitable, Mutual of New York, and New York Life. Counsel
for the Armstrong Committee was Charles Evans Hughes, a
man who could scarcely be considered prejudiced against the
companies. One of the conditions Hughes made before ac-
cepting the job was that, regardless of what might be revealed,
no criminal charges would be made as a result of the hearings.

By the time they were finished, the Armstrong hearings had
revealed a great many things—inordinately high salaries, nepo-
tism, excessively costly marketing practices, shady investment
and political activities, self-perpetuation of executives and
directors through proxy votes (one Mutual of New York
executive, Richard McCurdy, was found to have entered the
names of 300 nonexistent policyholders in the company rec-
ords so that he might vote their proxies).

Hughes' own report of the investigation stated that the Big
Three's "membership is so large and their resources so vast
as to make the question of responsible control and conserva-
tive management one of extreme difficulty and their management, if permitted to grow unrestrained, will soon become a
serious menace to the community." [11]

The Armstrong hearings in New York received nationwide
attention, and triggered a series of similar investigations in
other states, and in the process the true loyalty of many a
state insurance commissioner came to light. Wisconsin and
Missouri were among those who attacked the problem with

considerable vigor, while others went about it in a timid manner, as though afraid to rock the boat any further.

Insurance departments were created in several states where none had existed before, while others made the post of insurance commissioner elective rather than a political appointment. Several years after the investigations it was estimated that more than 1,600 insurance bills had been introduced into the various state legislatures, but by that time the storm had died away, and only a small fraction of these became law.

The third of the nonforfeiture values, that of guaranteeing a Cash Surrender Value upon terminating a policy, began to crop up purely as a competitive sales device at about the turn of the century. There was no legal requirement for this feature, and therefore no uniformity from state to state. The important thing was that, even though the allowance of cash and loan values was far from equitable, the provision had at least been introduced. This, along with the airing that had been given the industry, restored public faith in life insurance to a considerable degree.

Following the First World War, and through the prosperous twenties, vast amounts of life insurance were sold. When the Depression struck in 1930, the income of life insurance companies in the United States greatly exceeded that of the Federal Government.

But the thing that has always been feared by the industry began to happen. Policyholders by the thousands sought to extract the cash from their policies, either by loans or by surrendering the policies. In February, 1933, an unpublicized meeting of top life insurance company officials and state insurance commissioners was held in New York, its purpose to arrange a moratorium on all policy loans and cash-surrender payments.

The insurance commissioners balked, pointing out that such a moratorium was clearly illegal. Since any action of the sort would have to be taken by the commissioners and not by the companies, no action resulted at the time. Then came the 1933 moratorium on the nation's banking, and the life insurance industry was able to climb aboard the lifeboat. Two days after the banks closed their pay-out and pay-in windows, the life insurance industry, working through state commissioners, declared a moratorium of its own which lasted six months.

There was a big difference, however, because the life companies kept the pay-*in* windows wide open. In those desperate times many people made almost any sacrifice in order to keep their life insurance in force, and premiums continued to flow in.

The life insurance industry was a paradox during the long years of the Depression. It swam against the tide. From 1929 through 1934, while stocks depreciated from an average of $228 to $32 per share; while industrial bonds dropped more than $12 billion in value; while 10,000 banks failed, and governments all over the world defaulted on international debts, the assets of life insurance companies steadily *increased,* from $18 billion in 1929 to almost $23.5 billion in 1934.

Policies lapsed by the millions, more than 20 million in 1934 alone, amounting to some $4.4 *billion* in insurance protection. The reserves on these policies remained with the companies, and during the Depression years were estimated at more than $750 million.

The need for guaranteed nonforfeiture laws grew even more apparent as the Depression ended. The industry continued to drag its feet, and it was not until after World War II, in 1948, that a uniform, nonforfeiture law was fashioned, and passed by all the states. The guarantee of Cash Surrender Values after three years on ordinary life insurance, and after five years on industrial life insurance, at last officially established the "savings plan."

The Cash Surrender Value now heralded by life insurance

men as the "first and foremost savings plan ever devised by the human mind" is, then, nothing more than the final form of nonforfeiture against which the industry had fought for more than a century.

Chapter 5

The Cost Is Prohibitive

"Avoiding 'prohibitive' costs at advanced ages can be seen to be impossible, for the increase in mortality is actually paid for by each policyholder. In level-premium insurance, you merely agree to make substantial overpayments towards a fund to decrease steadily the 'net amount of risk.' "

—Philip Gordis, *How to Buy Insurance*

The foundation upon which the infinitely and unnecessarily complex structure of American life insurance is based is the mortality table, a statistical record of the death rate among Americans. The mortality table reflects the number of persons per thousand of each age group from birth to age 100 who will die during any particular year. From these figures, life insurance actuaries compute premium rates. From the outset this is loaded in favor of the companies. The tables are based on past experience, while life insurance death claims are themselves a factor of the future. The life expectancy of Americans, through advances in medical science, better living conditions, and other factors, grows longer each year.

The latest mortality table in use, the Commissioners Standard Ordinary, 1958, called the CSO 1958, is based on the American death rate for the years 1950–1954. The raw material of a mortality table is the mortality cost, that is, the amount of money that must be supplied by the survivors of any age group to meet the death payments of those who will die.

For example, the table shows that 1.79 individuals, age 20, of a group of 1,000 will die during that year. Therefore, assuming each has a policy of $1,000, there will have to be

$1,790 to meet these claims. Each of the 1,000 would have to supply $1.79.

Over and above this basic mortality cost is the tremendous financial "load" of the companies—the high sales commissions, home office expense, costs of conventions, sales awards, and so on. Even with the inclusion of this "load" factor, the actual premium rate for a 20-year-old person is still far from being prohibitive. It is at the other end of the life span that the cost becomes prohibitive. As one writer put it, "A life insurance rate could be calculated for a man age 98, but no one would be likely to pay it." [1] The mortality cost at age 98, according to the same table, is $668.15. For age 99—at which the mortality table assumes the last of the group will die—the cost is $1,000. Obviously, no one would consider paying these prices—which would be higher with the addition of the "load."

Herein lies one of the most baffling paradoxes imaginable. It is apparent that no one would pay such prohibitive costs for life insurance, yet more than 120 million Americans *are* paying these costs with every premium payment mailed to their life insurance company. This could explain why the level-premium concept has been called one of the most ingenious mathematical devices ever conceived.

In order to calculate a level-premium payment, the mortality costs for the entire life span to age 100 have been pooled, leveled, and from this the premiums drawn. Regardless of the age at which an individual buys level-premium, permanent-type, Cash Surrender Value life insurance, *his very first payment and all that follow* pay a portion of the prohibitive cost of later years.

The possibility of total price disclosure in permanent life insurance is of grave concern to the industry. If the public becomes fully aware of the fact that all permanent-type life insurance is nothing more than decreasing-term insurance

coupled with a "savings" feature on which the policyholder
gives up interest he should be earning, and that he is paying
premiums in advance over a life span that is actuarially calculated to end at age 100 (whether the policyholder himself
reaches that age or not), then trouble can be expected from
policyholders.

This fear of allowing people to know what they are paying
shows itself in life insurance publications from time to time.
The *National Underwriter,* in reviewing a recently published
book which purported to expose the industry, dismissed the
book as harmless, but went on to wonder "whether the founda-
tions might be shaken if someone ever blew the whistle." [2]

The View from Front and Rear

Interpretations of precisely what is accomplished by the
level-premium concept of "permanent" insurance can be as
confusing as the idea itself. Who benefits, if anyone?

Is it the beneficiaries of the man who dies prematurely, or
is it the man who lives to old age? Life insurance men approach it from whichever end is convenient. Griffin Lovelace,
quoted elsewhere in this book, wrote that "the fortunate
policyholder who is alive at age 65 has paid his share of the
death claims of the unfortunate ones for the benefit of their
widows and children." [3]

Mehr and Osler, in an insurance text, cite the virtue of
the golden calf by approaching from the opposite end, stating
that "premium payments above those required . . . made
by those who die young are used to level the premiums and
pay the death claims of those who live a long time." [4]

This knowledge would give little solace to a young man
who had been sold a policy on which there were premium
payments above those "required," and which provided inadequate death protection for his widow and children so

that the death claim might be paid on some old man 40 or 50 years in the future.

In both instances the true purpose of life insurance has been lost in the fast shuffle of words. A life cannot possibly be insured. Death is inevitable and the only aspect of death that can be insured is the uncertainty of when it will take place. It bears repeating that life insurance ("death protection" is a far more apt term) can reasonably do one thing, and that is provide for the future economic value of a man should he meet a premature death. With each year that passes a man has that year's economic experience behind him. The income earned and the expenses paid are both in the past, therefore he does not need to continue insuring against the loss of his economic potential for that year. Furthermore, a man whose children are grown and earning their own livelihoods no longer has the responsibility of insuring against the possible loss of his future economic value to them.

As shown in the two examples in the introduction of this book, the difference between buying pure death protection and buying any form of so-called "permanent" life insurance can mean the difference between leaving a family financially secure and leaving it insecure. The level-premium concept of "permanent" life insurance has *not* done away with the utterly prohibitive costs of life insurance at older ages. It has merely made these costs appear to be more palatable. What it has actually done is place a severe burden on the man who finds death protection a necessity, and that is the man who has others dependent upon his breadwinning capacity.

By age 65, the economic responsibility of a man to his dependents is, in the vast majority of instances, fulfilled. He has little or no need for death protection. Yet, using the mortality table upon which premium rates are based, we find that of the 100-year life span it assumes, *only 8 percent of the mortality cost is from age 0 to 65, while the remaining*

*92 percent is from age 65 to 100, or the years when the need
for life insurance has greatly diminished or disappeared entirely.*

It is this 35-year span of utterly prohibitive cost that causes
most young men with family responsibilities, who die a premature death, to leave their beneficiaries in financial straits.

No Less Prohibitive at Younger Ages

A favorite foot-in-the-door gimmick of life insurance salesmen is: "Buy it when you're young, it costs less." It would
make as much sense for a car salesman to say, "Finance your
new car over five years instead of three, it costs less." It
doesn't cost less; it simply lowers payments by spreading them
over a longer period of time.

Calculating life insurance premiums is not as simple as
figuring the monthly notes on an automobile, but there is an
analogy. A man buying life insurance at the age of 20 will
pay a lower premium than the man buying it at age 30, simply because he is expected to pay these lower premiums over
a longer period of time.

The real advantages of buying life insurance at younger
ages are (1) to provide immediate death protection and (2)
to have this protection should anything happen to cause the
policyholder to become uninsurable.

Neither of these advantages calls for the purchase of "permanent" types of insurance. In summing up this and earlier
chapters, permanent types of life insurance should be avoided
for the following reasons:

1. As the Cash Surrender Value "savings account" rises,
   the death protection declines in direct proportion, taking
   the insurance company "off the risk" and putting the
   policyholder into the business of unknowingly insuring
   himself.

2. At the time of death, the beneficiary receives only the face amount of the policy, which can be interpreted in one of two ways: either the insurance company has paid the full death claim and retained the "savings account," or it has returned the "savings" and contributed only that amount toward the death claim necessary to make up the face amount of the policy. Either way, the beneficiary is the loser.

3. Throughout the span of the contract, whether this is until the policyholder's death or such time as he surrenders the policy, he has foregone interest on his "savings" feature.

4. The policyholder is required, through the level-premium concept of "permanent" insurance to pay the utterly prohibitive costs of life insurance at older ages—in *advance* —through the device of blending these costs into the otherwise lower costs at younger ages.

5. Sales commissions, taxes, and all other costs are figured not only into that part of the premium buying pure death protection, but also into that part going toward the "savings," or Cash Surrender Value.

Chapter 6

Getting the Cash from Cash Surrender Value

"Unpaid loans are deducted from what your beneficiary gets, but there is no corresponding reduction in the premiums you pay."
—*Changing Times*, April, 1967

There are three ways that Cash Surrender Value "savings" can be gotten out of a permanent-type life insurance policy in *cash*. We have already seen that the life companies legally and actuarially deny that the policyholder has any ownership of any part of the company reserves, including the Cash Surrender Value reserves, even though the exact opposite may have been a big part of the sales pitch that sold the policy. However, they will—in fact, they *must*—turn this money over to you in one of the following ways.

Part of the Death Claim

This method of getting the Cash Surrender Value "savings" has long been a source of mystery to people who could not understand how a man could "save" money with his life insurance company up until the very day of his death and then have the "savings account" somehow vanish when the death claim was paid. The death claim of permanent types of insurance is the face amount of the policy, whether the policy has been in force 10 minutes or 80 years, and no matter whether the Cash Surrender Value "savings" are one dollar or virtually the entire face amount of the policy.

Years ago one of America's greatest actuaries, Sheppard

Homans, criticized this oddity of level-premium, permanent-type insurance by writing:

> The companies are introducing a savings feature which, while it increases the cost of insurance, does not increase the protection. Therefore the companies should be compelled to open a double entry account for each policyholder. Then in the event of the insured dying before the investment part of his contract became effective, the company would be compelled to return to the beneficiary, in addition to the face of the policy, that amount he had placed with the company for the purpose he had failed to live to realize.[1]

Homans was saying very bluntly that the companies should pay the face amount of the policy *and* the Cash Surrender Value "savings account."

The Meaning of "Surrender"

A dictionary definition of "surrender" is: to give up or abandon. For the man who would like to withdraw his life insurance "savings" with no strings attached, there is one important string that must be cut. He has to give up or abandon his death protection. The policy itself must be surrendered to the company. If the man has become uninsurable since taking out the policy, the consequences of being forced to give up his death protection might prove disastrous for his beneficiaries. In many cases, however, where insurability is no problem, surrendering a "permanent" policy and withdrawing the Cash Surrender Value can be the wisest move to make. This will be thoroughly discussed in a later chapter.

How to Borrow Your Own Money

The third method of getting Cash Surrender Values can be most revealing. Any generally acceptable definition of the word "savings" would certainly include the fact that the savings belong to the individual doing the saving, even though the actual fund may be kept for him by another person or by a financial institution. Not so in the life insurance industry's confusing lexicon.

Even though the life insurance companies will not allow the withdrawal of Cash Surrender Values without surrendering the death protection at the same time, they will allow the policyholder to borrow his own "savings" from them. This borrowing is considered a loan, and a loan means that there will be interest to pay. The interest rate on life insurance policy loans is usually set at 5 percent. The policyholder, then, continues to pay the regular-level premium he has been paying all along, *plus* the interest on the loan the company has allowed him on his "savings account," which decreases his life insurance protection dollar for dollar.

As an example, let's take a man who has a $10,000 whole life policy, which over the years has built up a Cash Surrender Value sufficient for him to borrow $2,000. He makes the loan at an annual interest rate of 5 percent, and he does not have to pay off this loan so long as he lives and keeps the policy in force. The loan, just like any other loan, has to be repaid eventually. At the time of the policyholder's death the amount of the loan will be deducted from the face amount of the policy ($10,000 minus $2,000), and his beneficiaries will receive a death payment of $8,000.

This relatively simple transaction should shed a ray of light to anyone who owns Cash Surrender Value life insurance, for it becomes apparent that his level premium has always paid for a steadily decreasing amount of true death protection, and this decreasing death protection is represented by the difference between the face amount of the policy and the Cash Surrender Value in any given year. If he leaves the Cash Surrender Value in the hands of the company, he is losing interest he might otherwise be earning; if he takes the Cash Surrender Value out, he must pay interest to the company.

Significantly, the companies regard this use of "savings" by the policyholders as an investment made by the companies. In its 1966 annual report, Southwestern Life Insurance Company of Dallas, Texas, referred to its policyholders' withdrawing their "savings" during the tight 1966 money market as follows: "Southwestern Life policy loans showed a net increase of $8,593,543. representing nearly 8% of the company's total new investment for the year."

In other words, in this 8 percent of total "new investments," the company was lowering its "in force" life insurance by almost $8.6 million, coming "off the risk" for that amount, for these policy loans will eventually have to be paid out of the face amount of the policies involved. At the same time, the company goes on collecting the same premiums it had always collected on these policies, and in addition is taking in—from the policyholders—interest on the $8.6 million, which at 5 percent amounts to $430,000 a year.

In defense of this practice of the industry, the agency manager of State Farm Life's Peoria, Illinois, office, Mr. Ned Loar, Jr., CLU, stated in a trade journal: "I don't know of any bank that will continue paying interest on withdrawn savings accounts." [2]

Here again we run into the upside-down world of life insurance. Certainly a bank will not continue paying interest on withdrawn savings accounts. The question is, does any bank *charge* interest on withdrawn savings accounts?

Policy loans are a leading cause of lapsation, or the dropping of policies. Mr. Dudley Dowell, president of New York Life, touched on both ends of the policy loan business while addressing a life insurance group in 1966. Mr. Dowell said that "policy loans are one of the reasons the business was sold in the first place," then he grudgingly admitted that "borrowed life insurance is more subject to lapse." [3]

In order to understand the prime reason behind this, let's examine the case cited earlier in the chapter. Our policyholder has borrowed $2,000. The original face amount of his policy is now clearly reduced by $2,000, and perhaps it dawns on him that he has not really borrowed this money either from himself or the insurance company, but from his *beneficiaries*. Unless the loan is paid back before he dies, the payment will be deducted from the face amount of the policy at the time of his death.

The logical question arises: what would be the advantage in the policyholder's repaying the loan? He would, of course, have to accumulate the $2,000 in order to do this. Assuming he now has the $2,000, he could turn it over to the insurance company and the annual interest statement for $100 (or more) would stop. But at the time of his death, the same $2,000 would simply come back to his beneficiaries as part of the face amount of the policy. He might just as well have put the money in a savings bank, drawn interest on it and turned the interest over to the life insurance company. Either way he does it, it becomes obvious that his death protection has dropped, and his actual cost has risen—whether it be in interest paid to the company (in the case of his borrowing his "savings") or in interest lost (in the case of his returning the money to the insurance company).

Chapter 7

Other Nonforfeitures—
Paid-up and Extended Term

"Nonforfeiture Provisions: This is one of the best places of all to lead a man into a swamp of confusion! Instead of talking in the terms as set forth in the policy, a salesman can say something like this: 'Mr. Brown, this policy includes some wonderful guarantees.' "—Hugh S. Bell, CLU, *Up the Ladder to Bigger Sales*

Paid-up Insurance

The first thing to say about paid-up life insurance is that there is no such thing as paid-up life insurance. The term itself is just as misleading as the idea of Cash Surrender Value being a "savings" or "investment."

Paid-up insurance is one of the nonforfeiture provisions that was forced on the industry, a choice allowed the policyholder in the use of the reserve, or Cash Surrender Value, of his policy. Basically, this provision means that the owner of a policy that has Cash Surrender Value can at any time stop making direct premium payments to the company and buy with his Cash Surrender Value a paid-up policy. Generally this choice is exercised at retirement age, when the continued payment of life insurance premiums would be too great a burden.

As an example, let's take the case of a 65-year-old man who owns a $10,000 "whole" or "straight" life policy. On the average, this type of policy will have a Cash Surrender Value of approximately 50 percent of the face amount, or $5,000, when the policyholder reaches age 65. Among the choices open to our policyholder, assuming he no longer wishes to continue premium payments, is that of buying paid-up insurance with this Cash Surrender Value. Again, taking the average throughout the industry, at age 65 each $1,000 of Cash Surrender Value will buy $1,320 of paid-up life insurance. The key word here is *buy*. For the payment of a single premium—his $5,000 Cash Surrender Value—our policyholder receives a paid-up policy of $6,600, or 5 times $1,320.

By deducting the amount the policyholder has paid ($5,000) from the face amount of the paid-up policy ($6,600), it becomes apparent that he has bought only the difference—$1,600—as his death protection. His life insurance agent will, of course, point out that our policyholder is now forever free from having to make premium payments.

But is this true? Suppose he had elected to take the Cash Surrender Value in actual cash. He could, conservatively and without risk to the principal, have earned 4 percent, or $200 per year, on this $5,000. By turning the $5,000 over to the insurance company, then, he is foregoing $200 a year. Even though the money does not pass through his hands, he is paying $200 a year for $1,600 of death protection. Simple arithmetic shows that he is paying at the rate of about $125 per $1,000 for this protection.

If our 65-year-old man has any real need to protect his future economic value by buying life insurance, *he could even buy new "permanent" insurance for approximately half this amount per $1,000.*

The life insurance industry has taken the paid-up provision of nonforfeiture—which was forced upon it—and created a breed of paid-up policies. These are limited-premium-payment, such as ten-pay, twenty-pay, paid-up at age 65, and others which become "paid up" after the specified number of years or at the specified age. The same principle applies to these, and any other variation of permanent, Cash Surrender

Value life insurance. A policy can never be truly "paid up," for the policyholder is buying the so-called "paid-up" insurance with his Cash Surrender Value, and in so doing is giving up the interest on that amount.

Extended-Term Insurance

Extended-term, or continued-term, insurance was the first guaranteed nonforfeiture provision forced on the life insurance industry.

Extended-term, as described by actuary Joseph Maclean, provides

> continued temporary insurance protection of the same amount as would have been payable under the original policy, the period of insurance being such as can be purchased by the net cash surrender value when applied in a single net premium.[1]

Thus a policyholder who does not wish to continue premium payments, or who cannot continue them, is allowed the option of using his Cash Surrender Value as a single premium payment, for which he receives a level-term policy equal to the face amount of his "permanent" policy. The length of the term is specified in the policy itself, and depends upon the amount of Cash Surrender Value and the age at which the option is exercised.

For example, in the case of a 65-year-old policyholder whose $10,000 "permanent" policy had a $5,000 Cash Surrender Value, the single payment of a $5,000 premium (his Cash Surrender Value) will continue the face amount of the policy ($10,000) as extended-term insurance for approximately 15 or 16 years, varying somewhat from one company to another.

The wisdom of such a move depends entirely upon the indi-

vidual situation. For an individual whose health positively
indicates he cannot outlive the term period and who is uninsurable for new coverage, this option might be of value.

This nonforfeiture provision, when closely examined, reveals the pay-in-advance scheme of level-premium, "permanent" life insurance. The single premium paid by using the
Cash Surrender Value of the policy represents the amount of
money the policyholder has paid in advance, and the length
of the extended term itself reveals the time for which the
advance payments have been made. Therefore, the Cash Surrender Value of any "permanent" life insurance policy can
hardly be considered a "savings" or "investment"; a far more
accurate term would be simply "paid in advance."

The payment of a single premium for the extended-term
(which is *level*-term and, as a subsequent chapter will show,
not a good way to buy term insurance) means only that the
policyholder has been induced to pay in advance *again*. For
instance, suppose the policyholder who has paid his $5,000
single premium to keep the $10,000 level-term in force for
15 years dies the *first* year. He will have paid for 14 years of
protection which he did not receive, and the 14-year overcharge is automatically forfeited to the insurance company.

Once again the life insurance industry has managed to get
things going in full reverse, for what was supposedly intended
as a nonforfeiture provision has gone full circle and become
total forfeiture again.

On the other hand, suppose the man's health is good and
he lives through to the expiration of the extended-term coverage. He has simply bet the company double or nothing, and
by living even one day too long has lost.

Chapter 8

Life Insurance: Sideline of the Industry

"Who cares what the buyer thinks? It's our job to convince him of what we think."   —*Probe*

There are six words that are capable of angering the most even-tempered of life insurance men. These words are *buy-term-and-invest-the-difference*. For a number of years there has been a type of financial counselor who has been advising the public to do this, to buy term insurance and invest the difference in stocks, bonds, or mutual funds. By following this advice people have still had to buy life insurance from the life insurance companies, but they have deprived the companies of the thing they were out to corral in the first place—the *difference*.

Term insurance, or pure death protection, as we have already seen, does not have the high profitability that the myriad forms of "permanent" life insurance have. The life insurance salesman who sells term insurance is not only an object of disdain among his fellows; he is apparently a candidate for the poverty program as well. Writing in the *National Underwriter,* the general agent of John Hancock's Boston office said of the evils of term insurance:

> We hire young men right out of college who somehow manage to pass the aptitude test, and *whammo!* The young man tries to sell his contemporaries who have no money, so he winds up selling them term, or ordinary life with all kinds

of term riders. He just isn't eating, so we lose him. We don't like to talk about the percentage that leave us.[1]

What do these young men have to sell in order to satisfy their hunger and stay with the company at the same time? Apparently it isn't life insurance, for the only *true* form of life insurance *is* term insurance. They must do the very thing that the industry rails against so violently. They must begin selling the industry's version of buy-term-and-invest-the-difference.

The so-called "dual-licensed" agent—the man who sells term insurance and securities of one form or another—is not as interested in the insurance sale as in the "invest-the-difference," simply because the "difference" is where the profit is. The same is true of the man who sells "permanent" life insurance as a combination of insurance and investment. The part representing pure death protection is incidental to the excess premiums going toward the Cash Surrender Value "investment." For the life insurance salesman, the real commission dollars are in selling the "difference."

As an illustration of this, the following chart shows several "permanent" plans available from Franklin Life Insurance Company, starting with the "inexpensive" whole life and going up to a gold-plated 10-Year Endowment. Each is $10,000 face amount, for a man age 35. The sales commissions tell the story.

In contrast to the commissions shown on the chart, the same agent, selling a $10,000 Decreasing Term to Age 65 policy, would have made a first-year commission of $27.69. Since the death protection of *all* the policies shown is decreasing-term insurance, the bulk of the commission money obviously is not coming from the protection element of any of the "permanent" Cash Surrender Value policies.

There are some brave souls in the industry who seem ready to be realistic about matters. A few years ago a Canadian life insurance man suggested that the nonforfeiture section of the

Table No. 4

Name of Policy or "Plan"	Annual Premium	Commission Rate* (Percent)	First Year's Commission
Whole Life (Paid-up at Age 90)	$ 246.30	80	$197.04
Life Paid-up at Age 65	295.60	80	236.64
Endowment at Age 65	350.90	75	263.18
20-Payment Life	359.50	80	287.60
Income Endowment at Age 65	469.90	75	352.43
President's Protective Investment Plan	568.80	80	455.04
15-Year Endowment	692.40	50	346.20
10-Year Endowment	1,113.90	30	334.17

* New York State law limits first-year commissions to a top of 55%, which in part explains the reason that only a relatively few of the 1,700-odd life insurance companies operate in that state. At the other extreme, there are companies which pay as high as 116% first-year commissions.

policy should have two additional columns of figures—one showing the amount for which the company remained "on the risk" each year, and the other showing the Cash Surrender Value as the "investment account." He went a step further to suggest that the death claim be paid with two checks rather than one. This would allow the beneficiary to understand that the "investment" was *not* lost at the time of the policyholder's death.

The Canadian saw this as an ideal method of combating the "termites" (life insurancese for buy-term-and-invest-the-difference men). What he failed to see was that the cat was getting out of the bag—the death protection was being laid bare as that old devil, decreasing-term. This suggestion scarcely made it past the suggestion box.

As stated at the outset, this is not a "buy-term-and-invest-the-difference" book. The prime problem in buying life insurance is to be absolutely certain of having all the pure death protection needed before concerning yourself with what to do with the "difference"—assuming there *is* any difference. Why should life insurance be tied in any manner whatsoever to even a valid program of savings or investment? The argument of the life insurance industry, hoary with age, has always boiled down to "People will not save or invest unless forced to do so." In order to save, a man's income must exceed his expenses, and forced savings tied inextricably to his death protection can be, and often are, a disaster.

The idea of "buy-term-and-invest-the-difference," whether the two operations are kept separate or not, is a misleading concept from the start. It assumes that the buyer has set aside a definite sum which is to be divided between the purchase of life insurance and investment. This is the point at which the separation should be made. No "difference" should be considered when death protection is being sought. In other words, never combine your death protection with *anybody's* plan that includes *anything* else.

Chapter 9

What to Buy

"No agent, manager, general agent, or agency system can live very well on the commissions from only term insurance."— Edward B. Bates, President of Connecticut Mutual Life Insurance Company, quoted in *National Underwriter*

Every level-premium life insurance policy has at least one feature in common with all others, and that is the steady decrease in the protection element of the policy. In the so-called "whole" or "straight" life policy, for example, the protection decreases steadily until it disappears at age 100 (96 in policies issued prior to 1948).

An actuary, Oliver de Werthern, questioned this when he wrote:

Why should a man aged 35 pay $20 a thousand for insurance to age 96 when he certainly will not live to that age or need insurance after age 60 or 65. . . . Why should he be compelled to pay more than $10 per thousand at that age or be compelled to open a questionable savings account? [1]

The decreasing protection of life insurance is as it should be, for every year that a man lives the costs of that year— food, clothing, shelter, medical expenses, and so on—will never have to be met again; consequently, there is no reason for him to insure against the economic loss his death would have caused his family for *that* year.

It is also true that the cost of life insurance increases with each year as the man grows older. This fundamental fact is hidden in "permanent" life insurance by the payment of a level premium and the maintaining of a level face amount of the policy. This illusion, as we have seen, is caused by the decreasing protection being balanced by the questionable "savings account."

If the protection offered in all life insurance policies is the same thing—decreasing-term insurance—why not buy only the pure protection?

Decreasing-Term Insurance

The life insurance industry itself has pointed the way in helping decide which plan of term insurance to buy. In the so-called "permanent" policies we have found that, at best, the protection is only about half "permanent" at age 65. That is, on the average, most "whole" life policies are one-half Cash Surrender Value and one-half death protection at age 65.

The plans calling for higher premium payments are even less "permanent." For example, an expensive Endowment at Age 65 policy takes the company entirely off the risk as the Cash Surrender Value reaches the face amount and the protection drops to zero at age 65. This completely refutes the argument that life insurance should be held "permanently," or for the "whole of life."

Decreasing-term insurance, carried to the age of 65, is the recommendation of this book. It is geared to retirement age, allowing the death protection to decline as the need for death protection diminishes, and allowing for the cessation of premium payments when the need for death protection is past.

The primary object should be to obtain long-term decreasing-term insurance. For ages up to approximately 45, a plan generally called *Decreasing Term to Age 65* is the most economical buy. When the length of the term shortens to 20 years or so (as Decreasing Term to Age 65 does when bought by a man 45 years old), it becomes more prudent to change to a slightly different plan. From age 45 through 50, a 25-Year

Decreasing Term plan is generally best. After age 50, 20-Year Decreasing Term usually proves to be most economical. It should be kept in mind, however, that these should be dropped at age 65 (if not sooner) if no need for further death protection exists.

Whichever plan of decreasing-term insurance is used, it should contain the following features:

1. It must be convertible to "permanent" insurance at any time for the full amount of protection in force at the time, even though need for this provision would be extremely rare. If the policyholder contracted a terminal disease and the life span could be medically forecast with accuracy, it might conceivably be of some benefit to convert ("conversion" will be thoroughly discussed in Chapter 12) so that the insurance in force might remain level. It is important to note here that the annual decrease in the term insurance might very well be *less* than the increased premium needed to buy the "permanent" insurance, in which case it would obviously be foolish to convert. Each case would have to stand on its own merits in this respect.

2. The death protection must decrease to *no less than 20 percent* of the original face amount of the policy by the time age 64 is reached. This allows for the policyholder to convert for this amount of "permanent" insurance (as described in Item 1) if conditions warrant doing so. Incidentally, conversion to "permanent" insurance under such conditions is not intended as a recommendation of "permanent" insurance; it is simply because the companies will not allow the protection to continue as term insurance.

3. The rate at which the death protection decreases should be examined closely. Some decreasing-term policies call

for a lower premium than others. The cheaper price is often due to the particular policy decreasing more rapidly than a slightly costlier one.

The following chart shows a complete breakdown of a Decreasing Term to Age 65 policy (the example here is for a man age 35; appendix II contains similar charts for ages 20 through 55). The figures represent policies that are presently available through various life insurance companies. These are policies that *can* be bought. However, decreasing-term—just like any other policy—can be manipulated by the company or agent offering it; therefore, anyone contemplating its purchase should study the chart for his particular age with care.

Columns 1 and 2 show the policyholder's age and the years the policy has been in force.

Column 3 represents the death benefit payable at the *beginning* of the particular year.

Column 4 is the annual premium (including waiver of premium), while Column 5 has been added specifically to point out the basic and inescapable fact of *all* life insurance— that the cost must rise each and every year, and neither the leveling of premiums nor the naming of policies can change that fact.

In analyzing this Decreasing Term to Age 65 breakdown, a life insurance man (of the "permanent" persuasion) would be quick to point out that the 35-year-old man, when he reaches age 65 and elects to let the insurance go, will have paid in all that money and will have absolutely nothing to show for it.

The thing he will *not* point out is that the protection element of any life insurance policy, being precisely what was paid for in the decreasing-term policy, will show the same result.

The life insurance company has taken on the entire risk, in the form of pure, unencumbered death protection, and it has

Table No. 5

Male, Age 35 (Female, Age 38)
Decreasing Term to Age 65 (30-Year Decreasing Term)

1 At Your Age	2 Beginning- of-Policy Year	3 Death Protection	4 Annual Premium	5 Yearly Cost per $1,000	6 Year's Decrease in Death Protection
35	1	$100,000	$393.80	$ 3.94	$3,300
36	2	96,700	"	4.07	3,300
37	3	93,400	"	4.22	3,400
38	4	90,000	"	4.38	3,300
39	5	86,700	"	4.54	3,300
40	6	83,400	"	4.72	3,400
41	7	80,000	"	4.92	3,300
42	8	76,700	"	5.13	3,300
43	9	73,400	"	5.37	3,400
44	10	70,000	"	5.63	3,300
45	11	66,700	"	5.90	3,300
46	12	63,400	"	6.21	3,400
47	13	60,000	"	6.56	3,300
48	14	56,700	"	6.95	3,300
49	15	53,400	"	7.37	3,400
50	16	50,000	"	7.88	3,300
51	17	46,700	"	8.43	3,300
52	18	43,400	"	9.07	3,400
53	19	40,000	"	9.85	3,300
54	20	36,700	"	10.73	3,300
55	21	33,400	"	11.79	3,400
56	22	30,000	"	13.13	3,300
57	23	26,700	"	14.75	3,300
58	24	23,400	"	16.83	3,400
59	25	20,000	"	19.69	None
60	26	20,000	386.20†	19.31	None
61	27	20,000	"	19.31	None
62	28	20,000	"	19.31	None
63	29	20,000	"	19.31	None
64*	30	20,000	"	19.31	None
65	31	None*			

* Unless you have decided to convert the remainder as described in text.

† At age 60 waiver of premium no longer effective, premium charge for it no longer payable.

charged a fair price for assuming this risk. The protection bought and paid for by 30 years of premium payments has done precisely what it was supposed to do—it has provided protection of the policyholder's future economic value through the entire time he *had* a future economic value, and by virtue of there being no excess premium siphoned into a question-able "savings account," that protection has been entirely ade-quate.

Thus, again, it comes to the separation of two objectives—the financial protection of your family against your premature death and the building of an estate through saving and invest-ing money.

It would be interesting to speculate on the future of level-premium life insurance if the combination of savings and yearly renewable term insurance were to be accurately and forcibly (by law) separated. Odds are its future could be measured by the time it took policyholders to get to the com-panies and cash in their policies.

Why Not Level-Term Insurance?

Many well-meaning and knowledgeable people recom-mend 5-Year Renewable and Convertible Level Term policies. Five- or 10-year level-term policies may be acceptable in cases such as a constant-level debt or encumbrance that is to be covered with the death protection. In the field of long-range financial planning there is no justification for any level-term policy. These policies automatically put the policyholder into a pay-in-advance situation, as they are no more than a short-ened version of level-premium insurance, without the Cash Surrender Value.

Most agents who sell 5-Year Renewable Term do so know-ing full well their services as an "adviser" will be needed when the term runs out. Thus they have a recurring opportunity to put the policyholder into their files as one of those converted to "permanent" insurance.

In addition to the chance to make the "permanent" sale, most companies give their agents the full first-year commission on each of these renewals, and consideration for this expense is figured into your premium.

Who Says Buy Term?

It might come as a shock to a policyholder, especially after he has heard his life insurance salesman run term insurance down as being the wrong policy to buy, to learn that the life insurance companies themselves are the largest buyers of term insurance. There is an item in life insurance nomenclature called *reinsurance.* From a legal point of view reinsurance is necessary because the directors of a company have specified either in the by-laws or in a resolution that the company will not retain for its own account a risk on any one life greater than a specified amount. For example, a company might issue a policy for $100,000. If its retention limit is set at $25,000, the mortality risk on the excess $75,000 would be transferred to another company or companies in the form of reinsurance.

If the $100,000 policy is a very high-cost endowment, does the company reinsure by buying high-cost endowment? Definitely not. When the companies are buyers, not sellers, they buy the very thing that they discourage their customers from buying. They buy pure death protection in the form of yearly renewable term, which, in essence, is decreasing-term. The company might be extracting a premium of $40 or $50 per $1,000 from the policyholder for a high-cost endowment policy while, at the same time "laying off" a large portion of the death risk at only a few dollars per $1,000.

William J. Matteson, in his book *Life Insurance and Annuities from the Buyer's Point of View,* stated that "we do not

recommend any other than term insurance for any purpose."
In *Life Insurance Stocks: An Investment Appraisal,* Arthur
Milton wrote:

> You may ask—what kind of life insurance and how much?
> The answer is simple: that which gives maximum protection
> for minimum premium, and as much as you can afford in
> relation to the goal which you have set for yourself. Decreas-
> ing term is an ideal vehicle. . . .

Michael H. Levy, president and founder of Standard Security Life Insurance Company of New York, writing in *Pension and Welfare News* in February, 1965, said:

> It is this writer's firm opinion that all young family men
> should purchase term insurance for an amount adequate to
> replace the breadwinner's earnings to permit a widow with
> young children to have enough money to "keep going." Few
> people are aware of the economy involved in purchasing large
> amounts of term insurance.

In an interview in *U.S. News & World Report,* Benjamin
Graham, one of the country's best-known investment analysts,
was asked:

> Q. Do you consider insurance an attractive investment outlet?
> A. I think perhaps it makes more sense for a person to
>   carry term insurance—as protection—and put his in-
>   vestment funds in stocks and bonds.

The life insurance salesman is represented by his employer
as being an expert, a man who will understand your life insurance needs and tailor a program to fit those needs. The
truth is, few life insurance salesmen are experts in life insurance—only in the selling of it. They could scarcely be considered impartial, for they earn their livelihood from commissions, and the commissions on high-price "permanent"

plans are much more attractive than the commissions on low-cost, pure death protection, or term insurance.

How Much Life Insurance Is Needed?

The purpose of life insurance must be kept in mind when deciding how much is needed. That purpose is to replace the future economic value of a man to his family in the event he dies a premature death. So the amount of life insurance he needs should be based on the size of his family, and the life his earnings have accustomed them to leading.

The minimum coverage could be set out as follows:
a. Married man with one child $ 50,000
b. Married man with two children $ 75,000
c. Married man with three children $100,000
    And so on

Suppose a young man, father of three children, dies. He earned $10,000 a year in his job. The financial requirements of the family have now dropped by almost one-half—the expenses of the head of the house, a fact that is surprising but true. There are no more life insurance premiums to be paid; his clothing, food, auto, club, recreation, medical, dental, and many other costs are ended.

If he had owned a $100,000 Decreasing Term to Age 65 policy, and if the face amount of the policy had decreased to, say, $90,000, his widow would be able to invest this safely at 3 or 4 percent—bringing in $2,700 to $3,600 annually. Added to this would be her Social Security benefit of approximately $300 per month, or $3,600 per year. Her total income would, then, be up to $7,200, entirely adequate to continue the upbringing of her children in the fashion their father's income had accustomed them to without invasion of the principal amount left from life insurance proceeds—which could be "invaded" if necessary.

Chapter 10

The Objections to
Term Insurance Refuted

"Because Term insurance is the insurance element of *every* life insurance policy, it is the foundation of the entire industry. For this reason, we can dismiss as immaterial all the arguments against Term—arguments against Term are really arguments against life insurance itself!"
— William B. Rudd, CLU, *The Tail Wags the Dog!*

In an effort to secure term insurance, the would-be policyholder will find the first stumbling block in his path to be the life insurance salesman. The principal reason for this is that the agent is, in a very real sense, penalized for selling term insurance instead of the higher-priced so-called "permanent" types. The commission rate paid on term insurance by most companies is 10 percent or more lower than the rates paid on "permanent." In addition to the lower rate, the premium itself is always lower; thus the salesman gets a lower commission rate on a lower premium.

Secondly, for the man who sells term insurance, it is difficult to become eligible for trips, awards, and other forms of recognition for high-volume performance. Selling a million dollars in term insurance does not qualify a man for the Million Dollar Round Table, nor does $5 or $6 million.

However, these reasons for discouraging the sale of term insurance are not the ones presented to the prospective buyer. The salesman is trained to convince you that *you* are making a mistake in buying it. Some of these objections—and the rebuttal to them—are as follows:

1. Objection: Term insurance is not permanent. It offers only temporary protection, and you need permanent protection.

   Rebuttal: In the first place, just what is "permanent" life insurance? If the permanent factor means the building of Cash Surrender Values (and it must, for the actual protection in any policy, as we have seen, is all term insurance), then the so-called "whole" or "straight" life policies could be considered as half-permanent when the policyholder reaches the age of 65, since this is generally the point at which these policies have one-half Cash Surrender Value and the remaining half is death protection or term insurance. Following this reasoning, then, the even costlier policies, such as Endowment at Age 65, must be even more "permanent" than the less expensive ones. At age 65, the endowment, or the Cash Surrender Value, of this policy is equal to the face amount. As for the life insurance part, or the pure death protection, *it has disappeared completely.* The argument, then, for "permanent" insurance is not an argument for insurance at all, but for the mystical "savings" or "investment" supposedly contained in permanent insurance.

2. Objection: Term insurance builds up no Cash Surrender Values, or retirement funds.

   Rebuttal: Anyone who has read magazines over the past few decades has certainly run across the life insurance ad that explains how "living insurance" will help you retire on a certain number of dollars per month. Years ago, the ad specified $150 a month. Then the figure began to go up, to $200, $250, and it continues to rise. The hitch in this, of course, is that the man who bought that idea when it was $150 is just now coming to realize this "investment" in his golden years. It's too late for him to get in on the $300 monthly income, and the $150 is not adequate for what he set out to do.

In buying the high-cost insurance necessary to implement this plan, he has very likely deprived his family of the death protection needed for the intervening years. If he had died—and millions involved in such plans have died—the protection his family needed for the loss of his future economic value to them would have been drastically reduced. And what about his old-age "retirement" fund? The insurance company kept it. The Cash Surrender Value and the "retirement" fund are one and the same thing.

3. Objection: Term insurance never has any loan value.

Rebuttal: This objection is an extension of the previous one. The loan value of a policy relates directly to the Cash Surrender Value in any given year. Aside from the fact that this loan is supposed to be the same money that was called your "savings" when the policy was sold to you, and that interest is charged to you when you borrow your own money, there is a hidden danger in having this money available as a loan from the life insurance firm.

For whatever reason a loan is made on the Cash Surrender Value of a policy, it solves no problem. The death payment to the beneficiaries is reduced by the amount of the loan, and to the regular-level premium paid during the lifetime of the policyholder there is now added the burden of the interest that must be paid to the company. This added cost of having the use of your own money must be borne year after year, creating the possible need for future loans to meet it. A time eventually arrives when the loan value of the policy has run out. If the payment of premium and interest now cannot be met, the only way out is to drop the policy, thus cutting off the death protection remaining. If the policyholder has in the meantime become uninsurable, the damage done by this vicious borrowing circle is clear.

4. Objection: Term insurance never becomes paid up. When the end of the term is reached, there is no death protection.

   Rebuttal: A previous chapter has shown that there is no such thing as "paid-up" insurance, even though the direct payment of premiums to the company may have ceased. The so-called "paid-up" policy is simply bought by the payment of a single premium, and that premium is the total Cash Surrender Value of the policy. In return, the policyholder gets a certain amount of insurance, always at a rate far in excess of the actual mortality costs for his age. He, in turn, not only transfers his Cash Surrender Value to the company; he sacrifices the interest he could be earning on this money. The lost interest is, then, the annual premium he continues to pay for the remainder of his life.

5. Objection: The cost of term insurance increases each year, and becomes prohibitive at older ages.

   Rebuttal: This particular objection is based on a false

premise. The cost of *all* life insurance increases as the policyholder grows older, for there is no way of getting around the natural rise in mortality with age. Life insurance men can demonstrate this very simply with a pencil and a scrap of paper. In doing so, they take a *level*-term policy; that is, a term policy in which the face amount, or the pure death protection, remains constant year after year. The premium on such a policy *must* go up each year because the mortality rises each year. They compare this with the level premium of one of their "permanent" policies, in which the face amount remains the same each year, and the face amount of the policy continues level. They fail to point out, for obvious reasons, that the cost of the pure death protection in these latter policies rises year after year, because the death protection is merely the difference between the face amount of the policy and the Cash Surrender Value.

6. Objection: Term insurance is the most expensive way to buy life insurance.

   Rebuttal: This objection, again, ties in with the previous one in that the life insurance man takes the term insurance as *level* death protection from start to finish, and shows that even though the cost seems to be less in early years, it eventually becomes extremely costly in later years.

   In attempting to show that term is more costly, a life insurance salesman will perform a bit of legerdemain known in the business as "net costing." This is done simply by totaling all the premiums paid into a "permanent" policy over a period of 20 or 30 years, then comparing this with the then Cash Surrender Value of the policy, the difference between the two being the "net cost" of the insurance. The comparison is then made to the premiums that would have been paid over the same time on pure death protection, or term insurance. There being no Cash Surrender Value, this is supposed to indicate the great superiority of permanent over term.

In this simplified approach, however, the two most important features in calculating the true cost of permanent insurance have been omitted. One is the loss of interest on the Cash Surrender Value "savings" over the period being compared. The second omission is that the insurance man assumes, apparently, that throughout the period taken the policyholder is spending every dime of the difference between the premium on the permanent policy and that on the term policy. It is this *difference,* discussed earlier, which he is using to make what purports to be a highly favorable comparison in favor of the policy he *wants* to sell. It can be easily shown that by investing this difference in a safe medium, with fair interest being earned, the policyholder is far better off buying only term insurance to cover his need.

7. Objection: Few people will save unless forced to do so.
   Rebuttal: The facts belie this argument against term insurance. Millions of individuals all over America invest regularly and profitably in savings banks, stocks, bonds, mutual funds, savings

and loan associations, and seem to be doing so without any force whatsover other than their own drive. However, if you truly feel that you cannot save a dime unless a life insurance company puts it away for you and in a "savings" account that bears no interest, and which they inherit when you die, then no rational discussion can dissuade you.

In summing up the various objections life insurance men put forth to the purchase of pure death protection, or term insurance, beneath each of them lurks one overpowering fact. The profit for salesman and company alike does not lie in the sale of *pure* death protection, but rather in the "difference," the excess payments, that are hidden in the premiums for so-called permanent life insurance.

Chapter 11

What to Do about
Cash Surrender Values

"But because I took the cash value out of my insurance . . .
I'm going to do all right. If I had had the foresight to buy only
term insurance . . ."—Murray D. Lincoln, president of Nationwide Life Insurance Company, *Vice President in Charge of Revolution*

If you are one of the scores of millions who have fallen
into the "permanent" life insurance trap (the life insurance
companies, in fact, are holding more than $128 billion in
Cash Surrender Value reserves[1]), what should you do about
it? The answer is simple. You should take this money and
put it to work for you in its entirety. You should take stock
of precisely what you have, how much it is costing you, and
then set about straightening out your life insurance by the
purchase of pure death protection.

First, find out what your present situation really is. This can
be done by taking a sheet of paper and setting down the following six items:

1. *Face amount of all "permanent" policies.* Whether you
   have one or one hundred, set down the total, and
   include the face amount of any so-called "paid-up" insurance, for, as we have already seen, there is no such
   thing as "paid-up" life insurance.
2. *Total Cash Surrender Values of all policies.*
3. *Subtract total Cash Surrender Values (Item 2) from
   total face amount of all policies (Item 1).* This will
   give the actual death protection for which your company

or companies are "on the risk." In other words, this is
the true life insurance for which you are now paying.

4. *Multiply total Cash Surrender Values (Item 2) by 4
   percent.* Four percent is a realistic rate of net interest
   you could be receiving *if* you had your Cash Surrender
   Values in a savings bank or savings and loan association
   instead of lying fallow in your insurance "savings account" at zero percent. This lost interest, then, is a
   very real part of the cost of your present life insurance.

5. *Total yearly cash outlay for premiums on all policies.*

6. *Add annual cash premiums paid (Item 5) to interest
   being lost on Cash Surrender Values tied up with life
   insurance company (Item 4).* This is the true annual
   cost of your death protection. Your death protection is
   not the face amount of your policies, but the difference
   between face value and Cash Surrender Values (Item
   3).

What can the simple analysis of these figures show you?
Let's take an actual case handled by this writer in his capacity
as a long-range investment planner. Ed Smith (not his real
name) was 35 years old, a successful clothing manufacturer.
Over the years he had been sold 17 separate policies, all so-
called "permanent" insurance, in various life insurance companies from coast to coast. There was a conglomeration of
"whole" or "straight" life, a few 20- and 30-year endowments,
some paid-up at 60 and 65 policies, with a sprinkling of other
"special" types, all of which had been—and still were—highly
profitable to the agents and companies who had sold them.

They were not at all profitable to Ed Smith, as he soon
discovered. The total face amount of this portfolio was $90,-
000. The annual premiums paid by Smith were approximately
$2,400, or an average of $26.67 per $1,000, not an unusu-
ally high figure for "permanent" insurance.

However, on totaling the various Cash Surrender Values,

it soon became apparent that his death protection was no longer $90,000. The total Cash Surrender Value was $12,000, leaving the companies on the risk for the difference, or $78,000.

Smith, in addition, was losing interest on this $12,000. By cashing in the 17 policies he could retrieve the $12,000, deposit it safely in a bank and draw 4 percent interest, or $480 a year.

Then came the calculation that stunned Ed Smith. The $480 interest that the $12,000 could safely throw off would *buy more than $120,000 of Decreasing Term to Age 65.* The cost with one company for this amount was $470.56, or approximately $3.94 per $1,000. In addition, he would be free of the $2,400 in annual premiums he had been paying in cash for his previous decreasing protection—now down to $78,000.

He would have 50 percent more immediate, pure death protection than he previously had, and he would also have a bank account containing $12,000, available to him at any time without affecting his death protection. Furthermore, the $2,400 previously worked into his budget for life insurance premiums would be free for whatever Smith wanted to do with it. He could spend it or invest it. If he elected to put it back into life insurance—in the form of pure death protection —at the cost of $3.94 per $1,000, he could buy almost $610,000 of Decreasing Term to Age 65.

In other words, by releasing himself from the trap of permanent insurance, Ed Smith could replace $78,000 death protection with almost $730,000—over 9 times as much, and *it would not cost him one cent more than he had been paying before in cash and foregone interest.*

In this particular case, Smith took out the $120,000 in Decreasing Term to Age 65 at an annual premium of $470.56, and chose to plow the $2,400 a year—that had previously been going to the life insurance companies—back into his business.

Suppose, on the other hand, Smith had decided to invest this $2,400 elsewhere. Life insurance men, in showing the "net cost" of their product, add the total premiums over a given time. They do not figure interest on this money. For example, the $2,400 annual premiums Smith had been paying would be shown in a life insurance "net cost analysis" over the 30-year period from age 35 to 65 as simply 30 times $2,400, or $72,000.

However, if Smith invested the money for himself, it would be a far different figure, as shown below:

$2,400 a year at 3% compound interest for 30 years—$114,180
$2,400 a year at 4% compound interest for 30 years—$134,601
$2,400 a year at 6% compound interest for 30 years—$189,744
$2,400 a year at 8% compound interest for 30 years—$271,872

What if Ed Smith died soon after taking out this new $120,000 in pure death protection? His family would have the $120,000 death payment *plus* the $12,000 that had been withdrawn from the life insurance companies and put in the bank. The family then would actually have $132,000 in death proceeds.

The View from the Other Side

Replacement of old insurance with new is called "twisting" by the men who push "permanent" insurance. Originally, this applied to the replacement of one "permanent" policy with another similar one. The fact that the industry has applied the same word to the reorganizing of a person's long-range financial planning is nothing more than an attempt to make the replacement of "permanent" insurance with term insurance appear to be unwise.

The life insurance companies take a very dim view of anyone who disputes the wisdom of the salesmen who write their policies. Any mention of "replacement" can slow down the process of replacing the old "permanent" insurance. Robert B. Mitchell pointed out the possible difficulties in an editorial in the *National Underwriter*:

> If he [the agent handling the replacement] admits there is to be a replacement, the home office may ask him a lot of questions and thereby delay issuance of the policy. Maybe the policy won't be issued at all.[2]

"Twisting" has been opposed throughout the history of the industry, and seldom for any reason relating to the welfare of the policyholder. The companies whose policies you have would like you to come to them for advice on whether or not to replace the policies, especially if this replacement is to be term insurance for their lucrative "permanent" types.

There have been times when the "anti-twisting" efforts of the companies have backfired, however. One such incident involved a former President of the United States, Calvin Coolidge. Coolidge, in 1931, was a director of New York Life, and in a radio address broke his well-known silence by stating:

> Do not let anyone persuade you to alter or switch your policies without the best advice of the companies that issued them. Beware of the so-called "twister" and abstractor or agent who offers to save money for you by replacing your policy in another company.[3]

This "advice" of Cal's aroused at least one man to action. An insurance expert, Louis B. Tebbets, brought suit for $100,000 against both Coolidge and New York Life, seeking "compensatory and punitive damages" for the harm done his business, which was just this sort of "twisting" to save his clients money. The case was settled out of court.

The only kind of twisting that "permanent" life insurance

men bestow their approval upon is replacing term insurance with the costlier "permanent" plans.

If the salesman who handles your life insurance is an old friend or a relative, and you feel honor-bound to go to him with your plan to analyze your Cash Surrender Value policies with a view to taking out decreasing term and dropping the old policies, then do so. It is doubtful that he will use the simple method outlined in this chapter. He may prefer to fall back on his fellow "experts." They, too, have a formula for unraveling the facts, and for your perusal we include it here, in the precise form in which it appeared in the *National Underwriter*.

Beneath the formula are the "directions" for its use:

$$_{t+n}V_x' - \left(P_x' \cdot {}_nu_{x+t} - \sum_{r=1}^{n} {}_{t+r}d_x' \cdot \frac{D_{x+t+r}}{D_{x+t+n}}\right) <$$

$$_tV_x' + \left(1 - 10^{-3} \cdot {}_tV_x'\right) {}_nV_{x+t}^2 + i \cdot {}_tV_x'\left({}_{n-1}u_{x+t+1} + 1\right)$$

$$-\left(1 - 10^{-3} \cdot {}_tV_x'\right)\left(P_{x+t}^2 \cdot {}_nu_{x+t} - \sum_{r=1}^{n} {}_rd_{x+t}^2 \cdot \frac{D_{x+t+r}}{D_{x+t+n}}\right)$$

Mathematical formula for determining whether replacing an existing policy would probably work out to the policyholder's benefit: Valued at the end of the period chosen for observation, using select mortality and an essentially riskless interest rate decreased by income tax for the "outside" investment fund, the cash value of the replaced policy at the end of the period less the net premiums (after deducting dividends) payable during the period must be less than the cash value released at replacement plus the cash value of the replacing policy at the end of the period plus interest on the cash value released at replacement less the net premiums (after deducting dividends) on the replacing policy. It seldom is.

In this comparison the face amount of the replacing policy equals the face amount of the replaced policy less the cash value released at replacement. The formula was exhibited by E. J. Moorhead, actuary of New England Life, in his presentation as a panelist at a discussion of the replacement problem before the annual conferment luncheon of the New York City CLU chapter.[4]

There. Simple, isn't it? However, exercise care in its use. It just could be the formula for the H-bomb.

Chapter 12

The "Conversion" Game

"We make it attractive every way possible to convert the term, once the business is in force, by allowing full commission, volume, and convention and contest credit for conversions."
—Howard W. Kraft, Vice President,
Ohio State Life Insurance Company

"Conversion" is the word the life insurance industry applies to its approved way of "twisting" policies. The word conjures up visions of missionaries at work, and it has a far more respectable ring than "twisting." Yet, according to a definition given by insurance text authors, Mehr and Osler, the two words can be synonymous. Twisting, they wrote

> refers in general to misrepresentation in order to induce the policyholder to drop a contract he already has and replace it with a new one. The practice generally relates to dropping a policy in one company in favor of taking a policy in a different one, although twisting might also consist of inducing a policyholder to drop a policy in the agent's own company in order to take another one in that same company.[1]

Conversion specifically means "twisting" a term policy into a "permanent" policy. In talking the owner of term insurance into dropping it in favor of a "permanent" plan, however, there is often considerable omission of facts which lead to confusion or misunderstanding. For instance, would the salesman ever disclose *any* of the following facts to his client: (1) that Cash Surrender Value takes the company "off the risk"; (2) that level-premium life insurance is not level-*cost* life insurance; (3) that the true cost per $1,000 goes up steadily as the company comes "off the risk"; (4) that the policyholder foregoes interest on the Cash Surrender Value; (5) that if he borrows his Cash Surrender Value he has forfeited that amount of his life insurance policy's death protection, *yet* he continues to pay the premium on this forfeited amount *plus* interest on it as well; (6) that there is no such thing as "paid-up" life insurance?

These are just a few of the "errors and omissions" involved in the conversion of term death protection to so-called "permanent" life insurance.

When term insurance is insisted upon by a prospect, it is sold reluctantly, and the new policyholder is immediately set up as a future target for "conversion." A State Mutual Life salesman, Walter Greenblatt, revealed his plans for the individual who insists on buying term insurance. "If, after all my efforts," wrote Greenblatt in a trade paper, "term insurance is bought, I set up in my office files a term conversion reminder file . . . and, once a year, twice a year, or even on a quarterly basis, I can, within a few minutes, quickly review my term policyholders, and thus organize myself to set up conversions periodically." [2]

Term insurance is not the money-maker for company and agent that their "permanent" plans are. Therefore, the object is to get it off the books as soon as possible—by conversion. "The trick of making term pay," an article in *Forbes* pointed out, "is to induce policyholders to convert to permanent whole-life policies as soon as possible." In short, they regard term as a foot in the door, not as an end in itself. "I don't believe anybody can make a decent profit on term unless they convert it," says President W. Dawson Sterling of Dallas' Southwestern Life.[3] "They" incidentally, means the company, *not* the policyholder.

An ad run in *The American Agency Bulletin* by Occidental

Life Insurance Company of California told prospective agents of the way in which conversion could fatten their bank accounts.

> DOES CONVERSION PAY? It not only pays, but pays handsomely.
> *Example:* You sell a $25,000 Five-Year Convertible and Renewable Term plan to a man of 30. The first year commission is $66.87. You convert that plan in three years to Guaranteed Whole Life. The new first year commission is $302.05!
> . . . The original term sale and the conversion are both considered new policies at Occidental and carry top percentage commission. Know an easier way to pocket more first-year commissions? [4]

This sort of "twisting" not only has the complete blessing of the home office, but the pressure coming down from above on the salesman to get out and make "converts" is intensive. One company, Republic National Life, in a letter advising a field representative of unconverted term insurance in his bailiwick, tells him in no uncertain terms that if he doesn't get out and do something about it, they'll give it to another agent. A form is attached, at the end of which is this underlined statement:

> If this report is not received at the Home Office 15 days before the next anniversary date of this policy, this conversion offer will automatically be assigned to another field representative.[5]

However, when an agent goes about this "conversion" the other way round—that is, unburdening a customer of "permanent," high-premium, high-sales-profit policies—the company hackles rise. At the annual meeting and sales congress of the Indiana Association of Life Underwriters a few years ago, the reaction to such "twisting" appeared in the form of a resolution which promised stern measures for these offenders:

> Be it resolved that in view of the increasing replacement of permanent insurance by decreasing term insurance, the field practices committee be instructed to investigate such cases brought to its attention. Since this is an abuse by persons licensed to sell securities as well as life insurance, steps should be taken to revoke the life insurance license *where misrepresentation is proved.*[6]

Sniffing after a conversion deal, life insurance salesmen often appear to regard the policyholder as little more than a jackpot at the end of the rainbow. One of the specialists in this area is Franklin Life Insurance Company. Sounding off in the company house organ, *Franklin Field,* the salesmen often wax ecstatic over this mother lode. One agent said that conversions of Home Protector (a term policy that gets Franklin's foot in the door) "are like finding gold."

Another generalizes that Home Protector is "the finest contract that the Franklin Life agent has to offer his clients," then immediately sets out to take away this finest contract by "conversion" and winds up with his reason: ". . . most important, is that you as the agent will receive two full commissions."

A third Franklin man said, "Term insurance must not be sold for the sake of term, but for the sake of future conversion. Term insurance is frustrating since you are merely paying for the cost of protection and therefore you want to convert at the earliest possible time." [7]

The "logic" in the latter statement is enough to make Socrates take a spin or two in his grave. What *is* life insurance if it isn't *protection?* If you are fortunate enough to have term insurance, don't let your friendly life insurance agent come prospecting around your house for "conversion gold."

Chapter 13

How to Buy Your Pure Death Protection

"All my life I've known better than to depend on the experts. How could I have been so stupid . . .?"   —John F. Kennedy

Buying the pure product of the life insurance industry is not an easy matter. Pure death protection, or term insurance, is something the life insurance boys want to keep back there in the actuarial department until it can be dressed up in one of the countless disguises that allow it to emerge as highly profitable (for them), Cash Surrender Value, "permanent" insurance.

A well-known salesman for Massachusetts Mutual, Mr. Ewing Carruthers, of Memphis, Tennessee, revealed the motivation behind this in writing to his fellow salesmen in the *Insurance Field*. With complete candor Carruthers wrote:

> If you sell a million dollars' worth of term insurance these days, no matter what age you are selling, when it comes to paying your bills, you simply do not have enough money to stay in the life insurance business, especially in the manner of a man who is supposed to be looked upon as a leader in his organization, community and in his industry.[1]

It is not the intent of this book to drive indigent life insurance salesmen into a life of crime so that they can meet today's high cost of living. However, the welfare of the salesman could hardly be considered as the principal function of life insurance. The policyholders of America have been kept in a limbo of utter confusion so that the system might prevail, so that the vastly more profitable (for the company and the salesman) "permanent" insurance could be peddled without the hindrance of a much less costly, and vastly superior, product being noticeably on the market.

There is a way to get the term insurance you need, but the path is beset by pitfalls that have been field-tested for more than a hundred years. There are four basic phases involved, and these are:

1. Finding a company and an agent
2. Filling out the application
3. The medical examination
4. Taking delivery on the policy

In skeleton form the four appear simple. Actually, they are not, and we shall proceed to go into the details.

1. *Finding a Company and an Agent*

If you have a friend who has straightened his life insurance out by buying term, ask him for the name of the agent who handled the transaction.

An alternate method is to find a "dual-licensed" agent—that is, a man who sells both life insurance and securities. *Caution:* He will gladly sell you the term insurance, but he may also exert pressure for that all important "difference." Point out to him emphatically that you are going to take one step at a time, and adequate death protection is the first step. If he does not want to work with you on this basis, find another agent.

Assuming you have found a man with whom you can do business, tell him what you want. As explained in Chapter 9, you want Decreasing Term to Age 65. You want it (as shown in the tables of Appendix II) to decrease to not less than 20 percent of the beginning face amount by age 64, and this final 20 percent is to be convertible to permanent insurance without evidence of insurability so that you can "select against the company" if your health indicates that con-

tinued coverage—even on the high-cost permanent plan—
would be advisable. Incidentally, this "selection against the
company" has been anticipated by the companies themselves,
and the cost of it has been figured into the premiums from
the beginning—which is only fair and equitable for both the
company and the policyholder.

Finally, insist that the agent supply you with a sample
copy of the contract you have agreed upon, with yearly
breakdowns as shown in the tables of Appendix II. Compare the sample to our table for your particular age. If the
annual decrease in protection, the annual premium, and
the 20 percent remainder at age 64 show the proposed contract to be equal to, or *better* than, the tables, then you are
ready for phase 2.

2. *Filling out the Application*

At least one question on life insurance application forms
might seem irrelevant to the applicant. It goes something like
this: *Will the insurance applied for replace any present insurance?* Your first thought might be, "What business is it of
theirs what I do with my present insurance?" However, as we
shall see shortly, any falsification in applying for the new coverage could lead to trouble, and so the questions should be
answered fully and truthfully.

A "yes" answer to this question results in something more
than routine handling. Even if the company to which you are
making application is one of the growing number that be-
lieves in the sale of pure death protection, a "yes" answer to
the replacement question will allow the company whose policies are to be "junked" an opportunity to try to talk you out of
doing so. The following memo sent out to the agents of one
company shows what happens:

1. Whenever a replacement is indicated [by a "yes" answer],
   the application must be accompanied by Illustration Forms
   #LR-167 (buff) and #LR-267 (blue), copies attached.

[Author's note: These copies, detailing everything, are to be filled out in triplicate.]

2. A completed copy of Illustration Form #LR-267 (blue) must be submitted by the proposed insured to his present insurance company.

3. Also, three copies of Illustration Form #LR-367 (green) must be submitted by the proposed insured to his present insurance company. Upon completion of Illustration Form #LR-367 (green) by that company, they are requested to forward one copy to the applicant, one copy to——— Life and retain one copy for their record. The responsibility for mailing #LR-367 (green) to the other Company shall be that of the ——— Life General Agent.

4. It should be borne in mind by all General Agents and Agents that if the answer to question 12 or 16 on an application is stated falsely as "no" when it should have been answered "yes," the severest possible disciplinary action would result.

Not only might the applicant himself die of old age while all this is being shuttled through the mails; the agent stands a fair chance of facing a home office firing squad if he thinks you answered "no" while thinking "yes."

This cooperation between competitors is known as the "intercompany compact." It was originally intended to block the old-time "twisters" who replaced "permanent" with new "permanent," thus reaping the heavy first-year commission every year or so. In recent years the industry has found it highly useful in combating a more knowledgeable public which, in increasing numbers, prefers to unload the "permanent" in favor of pure death protection.

3. *The Medical Examination*

Legally, anything that happened to you medically, or any other way, prior to five years before applying for the policy is no business of the life insurance company. If there has been any serious medical history that took place less than five

years ago, whether physical or mental, which might interfere
with issuance of the policy, then you had better wait until
the five-year span has passed (if it is close) before making
application.

Again, do *not* volunteer medical information. Answer the
questions put to you by the doctor and do not elaborate on
your answers unless elaboration is in your favor.

Arrange for the examination to be made in the morning,
with no consumption of either hard or soft drinks the previous night, after a good night's rest and a light breakfast.
You are in top form then.

Do not try to get by with false answers, since the life
insurance industry works with a group known as the Medical
Information Bureau, located in St. Louis, Missouri, which
has a rather complete set of the files and cross-files dealing
with the medical histories of policyholders throughout the
country.

The application and the medical report (or reports, since
two examinations are often the rule for larger amounts of insurance, especially term insurance) are off to the home office.
Now all you have to do is wait.

4. *Taking Delivery on the Policy*

Your salesman calls and says the policy has come. Check
it over carefully to be absolutely certain it is correct in all
details. If you are satisfied with everything else about it, take
a look at a clause generally called the *Incontestability Clause*.
In the backward language of life insurance this means the
Contestability Clause, for it is during this period—which
varies according to the company from one to two years—
that the issuing company can contest the policy. If you should
die during this period, and anything about your application
for the insurance can be proved fraudulent, the company
reserves the right to deny the death payment and litigate the
matter. The only thing the company must do is return the
premiums paid if it "wins."

For this reason, unless you are absolutely certain there is no cause for contestability, do not be hasty in turning in your old "permanent" policies. In some cases it is wise to continue carrying the old insurance until the contestability period has passed. If necessary, take out policy loans to pay the premiums on your new Decreasing Term to Age 65 policy during this one- or two-year period.

A word of caution about timing: Always wait until the anniversary date of the policy to cancel it. In this manner you receive the maximum amount of your money back because this is when the Cash Surrender Value addition is made. This is especially true with so-called "participating" policies, since the "dividend" (actually a rebate, as will be explained later) is paid at the end of the year also.

The day will come when you are in the clear. You will have that $50,000 or $100,000 or more in pure death protection. Your premium payment conceivably will even be paid by the interest you will now be earning on the Cash Surrender Values that you have extracted and put to work for you.

But remember—your name now occupies a prominent spot in that little file on the salesman's desk marked *"Possible Conversions."* You're still on his prospect list.

Chapter 14

Group Insurance

"I have no prejudice against group . . . some of my best friends are group men, although I certainly wouldn't want my sister to marry one of them."   —A life insurance agency manager

Group insurance is a plan which provides for the insuring of a number of people under a single policy, usually without medical examination. In order to prevent selection of risks against the company all members of the insured group must have a common employer or other restricted association.

Group insurance, as long as it is *term* insurance, is excellent, and if any need for life insurance exists, it should be acquired whenever it is available. The cost is very low, and in many cases all or part of the premium is paid by the employer. Under a group policy certain occupations which on an individual basis would be considered noninsurable are covered.

The cost is low for several reasons. The fact that usually no medical examination is required eliminates that cost. A single master policy, with a single premium payment, covers the entire group, thus cutting out considerable clerical cost. One agent generally handles the transaction, there is a single commission, and this is usually on a lower rate than individual sales.

Group term, just like all other term policies, does not extract the excess payments required by Cash Surrender Value "permanent" plans. Finally, the Internal Revenue Service allows the premium on group insurance, in individual amounts up to $50,000, to be tax-exempt as income. That is, the premium itself is not considered as income to the individual.

There are several shortcomings to group insurance. The

individual has no control over the insurance; that is, an employer may drop the coverage or the employee may leave the company. In the latter case, the insurance can be continued *only* by converting it to a form of "permanent" insurance. The only reason for doing this would be if the individual is uninsurable and needs the coverage.

Another shortcoming is the limitation of coverage. The amount of death protection available to an employee under a group policy is generally predicated on his income.

Perhaps both these objections will be removed in the future, but until they are, group should be considered only as supplementary coverage.

Reaction of the Industry

Group term insurance is, to put it mildly, not popular with the men who push Cash Surrender Value "permanent" insurance. Criticisms of group term cover a broad spectrum. The *National Underwriter,* for instance, saw in it a danger to the relationship between the agent and the client:

> Group life insurance is over 90% renewable term form with no personal relationship between two individuals to exchange ideas of the need for death benefits, savings, emergency funds and retirement.[1]

The "exchange of ideas" here can mean nothing more than the opportunity for the salesman to make a pitch to sell "permanent" insurance.

Probe took a harder line in an article entitled "Wild Group Must Be Stopped." The editors referred to certain areas in which group term insurance was being sold as "nothing short of a racket against the public interest, and what may become a fatal illness to the life insurance business."

The selling of group term insurance did not originate with

life insurance salesmen. It began with insurance brokerage
firms which serviced the property and liability needs of corporations. That is the reason it did not get off to a flying
start with "savings," "investments," and all the rest, but simply as very reasonably priced, pure death protection.

The Group Twist

Group insurance proved far too popular to kill, and so
the "permanent" insurance men—that is, those who depend
solely on life insurance commissions for their livelihood—
are now trying to bring it around to their way of thinking.
Group insurance is going to continue to sell, they reason, so
get in on it. Sell group—*but* don't sell group term.

A full-page ad run by Occidental Life of California in
Life Magazine began as follows:

Now You Don't
Have To Die
To Cash In
On Group Insurance

Group insurance is great, except for one thing. The guy who's
insured is never around to collect when it pays off.

The ad then went into the old song and dance about "cash
values," the "permanency" of ordinary life insurance, and so
on. The idea is that the company pays for the pure death protection, or term insurance part of the deal, while the employee
pays the "savings" part.

Meanwhile, the company ran another series of ads in life
insurance trade journals pointing out the real advantage of
"Group/Ordinary." This was aimed at the salesmen who were
forced to sell group term simply because nothing else was
available. A full-page ad in *Insurance Field* did not touch on

the "advantages" of the new plan to the policyholder. It ran like this:

A BROKER OF OURS JUST BROUGHT US A GROUP CASE.

IF IT HAD BEEN STRICTLY GROUP TERM, HIS COMMISSION THIS YEAR WOULD HAVE BEEN $483.00.

IT WASN'T THOUGH. IT WAS GROUP/ORDINARY AND HE EARNED A FIRST-YEAR COMMISSION OF QUITE A BIT MORE.

$10,599.00.

Quite a difference, we'd have to agree. And more than a little enlightening as to why that broker went all out to sell the Group/Ordinary instead of the group term.

Others look on group term as a necessary evil, but use it as a foot in the executives' door. The chairman of the board of Dallas' Republic National Life, Mr. Theo Beasley, discussed this angle in an interview in *Forbes:*

Sure, group insurance is a hard row to hoe these days. But you've got to consider the subsidiary benefits like selling individual policies on key company officers that may run into millions of dollars in face value.[2]

And they don't talk "term" when they're selling key-man insurance.

A "Harmful" Development

The National Association of Life Underwriters and the Life Insurance Agency Management Association—NALU and LIAMA—in their fifth biennial field opinion study asked the agents, among other things, what they considered the most harmful life insurance business development affecting their interests.

Group insurance led the list, as it had on previous field studies. Term insurance and direct writing (that is, by-passing the agent) were also regarded as not being in the best interest of both agent and the public. The interesting thing here is how the public interest and the interest of the salesmen become tied so closely together. Some people might consider it odd that the public interest is served by turning over a larger premium than necessary to the salesman. Group, term, and direct writing undoubtedly have cut into the interest of the salesmen, for their interest is the commission they make, and these three areas cut them off from possible commissions.

The question, then, is not whether group term insurance is good. It is very good—*for* the policyholder.

Chapter 15

Insurance for Women

"I've got it. Why don't we make the heading, 'What Most Women Know About Life Insurance,' and then follow with 10 blank pages?"   —An Editor, *Diamond Life Bulletins*

The most pressing concern in the commission-oriented minds of life insurance men is not whether any particular group of people needs life insurance; rather it is how it can be sold to them. In this pursuit an almost endless array of gimmicks has been employed. One of the latest is aimed at the woman in search of a husband, and it may ultimately go down in some sort of record book as the Most Absurd policy of them all.

It is called the "Dowry Plan" and, as Miss Amy Vanderbilt commented expertly in her syndicated column on seating arrangements and other crucial matters, it "may be unique and sensible. It offers young women an opportunity to buy insurance for themselves while they are single, then transfer it to their husbands when they marry." [1]

Miss Vanderbilt completely overlooks the simple question of whether the young woman has any *need* for life insurance, or whether her future husband might not particularly care to have his bride unload a "permanent" insurance policy on him.

Far more sensible for these young women, if they have money, would be to put it in a true savings account, or if catching a husband is their goal, to spend it at the beauty parlor or dress shop.

Life insurance for women, in most cases, is not needed. When it is, it should never be tied up in the hocus-pocus of "permanent" Cash Surrender Value policies, but only in pure death protection, or term, insurance. It is important to remember that the true purpose of life insurance is to replace the future economic value of a person in the event he dies a premature death. If there is no one to whom that future economic value is necessary, then there is no need for life insurance.

The following are, generally, the circumstances under which women do or do not need life insurance:

Single Women

1. *Single, unemployed, with no dependents.*
   Assuming, of course, that the unemployment is voluntary, that she does not have to work, there is no conceivable need for death protection. Any money spent on life insurance premiums is money wasted.
2. *Single, employed, with no dependents.*
   The same applies here as in Item 1, with the possible exception of her taking enough group term insurance through her employer to handle final expenses in the event of death. It should be stressed here that group term *only* is recommended (as covered in Chapter 14). If the company has been sold a group ordinary policy, then go to an individual basis and buy decreasing term.
3. *Single, employed, with dependents.*
   This situation calls for all the group term insurance available through her employer, with the possible addition of individual Decreasing Term to Age 65 in sufficient amounts to replace her future economic value in the event of a premature death.

Married Women

1. *Childless married woman who works.*
   A few thousand dollars in group term insurance is

sufficient here, but if the group term calls for a payroll deduction, it should not be taken if the money must be subtracted from any planned death protection on the husband. The basic family rule for life insurance is *complete death protection coverage on the head of the family* before considering any on the wife.

2. *Married woman who supplies entire income for family.* Here again she should avail herself of the maximum amount of group term insurance she can get through her employer. Generally, in the case of a mother who is the sole support of a family, the financial situation is extremely tight. However, the cost of Decreasing Term to Age 65 is very low, and if at all possible, this should be bought in whatever amount can be managed.

3. *Housewife with children.*
It is the housewife in a family with children who is the real target of the sharpshooter salesmen, for the simple reason that she is obviously in a situation where money is more likely to be available. A longtime life insurance man, M. Albert Linton, wrote that

life insurance on the lives of wives has a great value from the family point of view. The death of a wife may result in large bills for last illness expense. Where there are children, the continuing problem of maintaining the home is sometimes difficult. To employ someone for the purpose might involve a larger outlay than could be accommodated by the budget.[2]

The first point made by Linton, referring to the large medical costs possibly resulting from the woman's final illness, seems to be a far stronger argument in favor of hospitalization insurance than for life insurance. The medical bills will be there whether she lives or dies, and the life insurance will pay off only in the latter case.

Unfortunately, the author contents himself with telling only half the story. *Any* member of a family—wife, husband, child, even a pet—incurs expenses while alive. There are the basics of food, clothing, and shelter, and the endless other things from beauty parlor to dental bills that will no longer have to be paid for after the person's death. From the financial point of view, the family expenses, even if someone must be employed to look after the children and the house, will very likely be lower. As we have already pointed out in the case of the father's death, the family budget can be as much as 50 percent lower than it was before, without lowering the family's accustomed style of living. The same, to a lesser degree, is true of the wife.

Therefore, life insurance on the housewife is hardly necessary, and should not even be considered until the husband has all the pure death protection needed, and perhaps even more than is considered minimal. If, after this primary need is taken care of, it is still felt that the premature death of the wife will cause a financial setback, the Decreasing Term to Age 65 should be taken out on her in whatever amount is deemed necessary.

As an example of the low cost of insuring a woman of 30 who has several children and whose absence might incur added costs in raising them, $20,000 of Decreasing Term to Age 65, at $3.70 per $1,000, would cost only $74 a year. If any doubt exists in the family as to the wisdom of taking out insurance on the wife, the almost negligible cost would make it possible to have the coverage and remove that doubt.

Generally speaking, selling wife insurance is lagniappe for the life insurance salesman. One happy life insurance man, in the never-ending advice they bestow upon each other in the trade journals, writing about the easy relationship with the new policyholder at the moment of delivering a policy, concluded: ". . . his guard is down. . . . What better time will we ever have to discuss an educational fund for his children, or protection for his wife." [3]

Keep your guard up, Mr. Policyholder, keep your guard up.

Chapter 16

Kiddie Kontracts and the Family Policy

"... capture the baby market. ..."
—Advice of a life insurance trade journal

The scene is the home of Mr. and Mrs. John Jones. Martha Jones, at home alone with her three-week-old baby, is hanging the last of two dozen diapers on the line and praying it won't rain. There's formula to make, bottles to sterilize, the usual household jobs—vacuuming, making the beds, washing the breakfast dishes. ...

At that moment the telephone rings. Martha hurries into the house and lifts the instrument.

"Good morning," says a friendly voice. "Is this the John Jones residence?"

"Yes."

"Is this Mrs. Jones?"

"Yes."

"Martha?"

"Yes." (At this point she *should* frown suspiciously.)

"This is ＿＿＿＿ ＿＿＿＿, associated with ＿＿＿ Life. We understand congratulations are in order. Is this correct?"

(At this point Martha would do well to hang up. Instead:) "Well, yes, we have a new baby."

"How are you and the new boy (or girl) feeling?"

"Just fine."

"Swell! Is this your first baby?"

"No, it's the third."

"Two boys and a girl?"

"No, three boys."

"That's fine. Is John home?"

(At this point Martha should [a] hang up or [b] lock the door. Instead:) "No, he's at work."

"Fine, where does he work?"

"———— Steel." (Martha, apparently, is a pathological question answerer.)

"Well, Martha, we're reserving a baby book for you and John to keep a record of this new boy. We'd like to bring it around and get acquainted with you and John when it's convenient for you. Would this evening at six be convenient, or would ten tomorrow be better?"

"Well, six is just at suppertime; seven-thirty would be better."

"Fine. I'll see you at seven-thirty. Good-bye."

The telephone conversation you have just read appeared in an insurance sales manual entitled *223 Effective Approaches,* under the chapter heading "Educational and Juvenile." [1] (I shall mercifully spare you the other 222.) Life insurance salesmen have found a bonanza in selling high-profit "permanent" insurance on the lives of children, and they work at it with the relentlessness of a sourdough panning his way through the Klondike.

The only detail they overlook is the fact that there is absolutely no reason for death protection to be carried on the life of a minor, dependent child.

Not only is insurance on children sold by the billions, but in a great many cases it has the tragic result of reducing the death protection on the member of the family who truly needs it—the breadwinner.

Catherine B. Cleary, executive vice president of First Wisconsin Trust Company *and* a trustee of Northwestern Mutual Life Insurance Company, described the practice this way:

> In many cases . . . insurance is purchased on the life of
> a minor child when there seems to be inadequate insurance
> on the father's life. In my experience, the worst abuse in this
> area is on the lives of minors sold for their college education.[2]

The father very definitely needs death protection. But what
reason can be given for insuring his children against premature death? The economic value of a dependent child is neg-
ative. The child does not produce income upon which the
family is dependent; he costs money, as any parent knows.
Regrettably, the life insurance industry has successfully attempted to create in the minds of parents (and grandparents)
the belief that life insurance can send the kids through college. They make a strong emotional pitch, combining the
welfare of the child with the implication of delinquency on
the part of the parents (or grandparents) if they do not buy
life insurance for this purpose.

Let's examine a typical approach. Sears Roebuck, through
its Allstate Life Insurance Company, pushes a policy called
the Allstate College or Career Policy. A full-page ad in *Newsweek* says: *"Buy a $2000 Life Insurance College Fund for
Your Child—$13 a Month."* [3]

The child, a boy 5 years old, can cash the policy in for
this amount when he is 18. (Here, again, we see what Cash
Surrender Value means. The policy, and the death protection
with it, must be surrendered in order to withdraw the "savings.") The question arises: what was the point of the death
protection on the boy in the first place? If the child dies, he
obviously cannot go to college. If he lives, the part of the
$13-a-month ($156-a-year) premiums that went to pay for
the pure death protection portion of the policy was wasted.

If, on the other hand, the father wanted to provide a college fund, and was able to put $156 a year toward this goal
over the same 13-year period, he would have fared far better

by simply putting the money into an interest-bearing account at his bank or savings and loan association. The life insurance companies, in figuring an example such as this, will point out that the father paid into this "plan" just $156 a year for 13 years, or a total of $2,028. This, they say, is only $28 more than the amount that can now be "withdrawn" ($2,000).

Customarily, they avoid any mention of interest lost on the money during the 13 years. By figuring the interest at a realistic 4 percent, quite a different picture emerges. When the child reaches age 18, a true savings account would contain $2,594, or approximately 25 percent more than the Sears Roebuck "plan" would have provided.

Therefore, what possible reason can anyone have for tangling up a totally unnecessary life insurance policy with a plan to save money for a child's college education—especially when this entanglement reduces the funds available at the time the child is ready to enter college?

The life insurance industry has an answer of sorts to this. Suppose, they say, Junior *doesn't* go to college. By taking out the policy at an early age (5 is definitely an early age, even though life insurance salesmen lurk about maternity wards to "capture the baby market" even earlier) you will allow the child to continue paying for his "permanent" life insurance at the same low rate at which you started him. This, as we have already seen, is a specious argument. Life insurance does not "cost less" by virtue of having been bought at a younger age. It simply means the company intends to collect a lower premium over a longer period of time.

Forbes pointed out that, as of June, 1966, a minimum of $4,000 a year was needed to keep a child in an Ivy League school, and at least $2,000 a year in the big state universities. It suggested that the ten-year, 3 percent loans available under the National Defense Education Act for those who qualified, or bank loans for those who did not, might present a partial solution to a perplexing problem. *Forbes* went on to offer this sound advice: "In short, there's no easy way, and beware of the insurance or securities salesmen who tell you there is." [4]

Why does the industry continue to push this area of unnecessary insurance when it is so patently against the interest of the people who buy it? The life insurance newsletter *Probe* hit that nail on the head when its editors asked the musical question:

> Want to write a million [dollars] a year of the kind of business that will qualify you on all counts for the Million Dollar Round Table? [Author's note: There goes term insurance out the window.] Here's a simple sales talk that will do the trick. [5]

Probe showed a good command of the language by choosing the word "trick." It advised salesmen to approach the the grandparents of a youngster and use this pitch:

> I came to talk to you about your grandson, Bobby—because there is something you can do for him that could never be done until recently. It's a new type of life insurance coverage for youngsters.

Probe's prescription for a million dollars in sales a year was to find two such grandparents a week, and *voilá!*—there's the million. Did Bobby have any *need* for life insurance, even in the form of pure death protection (which it wasn't)?

They didn't go into that. But it is big business. One company, Metropolitan, tells us: "Four and a quarter million is a heap of teen-agers, and that's how many Metropolitan Life insures."

And that doesn't include the sub-teens *or* the more than 1,700 other life companies.

The Family Package

At a recent point in the unnatural evolution of life insurance a mutant known as the "family package plan" appeared. This automatically covered Mom and all the kids with term insurance *if* Dad would buy a "base" on himself of "permanent" Cash Surrender Value insurance. The protection on Dad was minimal, and the term insurance on the rest of the family was represented as being free.

Allstate, climbing on this bandwagon, described its version in the following manner:

> Get a $16,000 family package of life insurance . . . $17 a month. Allstate offers life insurance values in the Sears tradition—just what the young family needs. Say you and your wife are both 25 years old, and have one child. At Allstate you get $10,000 of permanent life insurance; your wife gets $4,000 of term insurance; and your child gets $2,000 of term insurance. And as your family grows, new babies are insured automatically—at no extra cost—when they're 15 days old. This is Allstate's Family Plan Package. Your cost? Just $17 a month. Isn't this the kind of life insurance you should have?

The answer to Sears Roebuck's question is a resounding *no*. And the reason is simple. The $17 a month ($204 a year) that the 25-year-old father is asked to spend in spreading his life insurance thinly over the whole family—with himself burdened with a "permanent" Cash Surrender Value policy of $10,000—would buy a completely adequate amount of pure death protection if applied to himself alone. An annual premium of $202.24 would buy a beginning amount of $60,-000 of Decreasing Term to Age 65 on *his* life.

It seems that even Sears Roebuck would have to admit the young woman and her child would be somewhat better

off with $60,000 than they would with $10,000 should the
breadwinner of the family meet a premature death.

Pan-American Life Insurance Company, of New Orleans,
is another of the scores of companies that have taken this
family package plan to their bosoms. In a recent full-page ad
in *Newsweek* (an ad that surely must have backfired in the
minds of thinking people) a family portrait of a man, his
wife, and 15 of their 17 children was featured. The lead-in
of the ad asked this question: *"$21,700 of Life Insurance for
only $149.21 a year?"* and emphatically answered. *"Yes!
That's what the _____ _____ family gets from Pan-
American Life!"* [6]

A close look at this "plan" does reveal that Mr. _____
got something from Pan-American Life—just *what* is debat-
able. Here's the breakdown on PALIC's "Wife and Dependent
Children Benefit Agreement":

> $3,500 permanent Cash Surrender Value insurance on
> Mr. _____.
> $3,200 term insurance on Mrs. _____.
> $1,000 term insurance on each of the children under age 18,
> or $15,000.
> Total on entire family: $21,700.
> Annual premium: $149.21.

A "plan" such as this completely ignores the real purpose
of life insurance, the protection of the future economic value
of the breadwinner in the event of his premature death. Pre-
sumably, Mr. _____ is the breadwinner in this case. Should
he die, this policy will pay his beneficiaries—*all 18 of them,
counting the two children over 18 and in college*—the sum
of $3,500. This works out to a little less than $200 each.

Mr. _____, who from the picture in the ad appears to
be about 40 years old, could have done quite a lot better
without the "advice" of the Pan-American Life salesman.

For example, at age 40 for the same outlay he *could* have bought almost $30,000 in pure death protection, Decreasing Term to Age 65, and placed it all where it belonged—on himself.

Chapter 17

Mutual Companies

"Not mutuality, but personal business selfishness created these companies."
—Dr. J. Owen Stalson, *Marketing Life Insurance*

There are two kinds of life insurance companies: stock companies, which are owned by stockholders, and mutual companies, which are supposedly owned by the policyholders. The stockholder-owned life insurance company, like any other investor-owned company, is expected to make a profit. The mutual life insurance company, however, with *no* stockholders rightfully expecting a return on their investments, theoretically makes no profit, and supplies life insurance at cost to the policyholders in the cooperative venture.

Theory and fact, in this case, are as far removed from each other as the North Pole from the South. In his book *Life Insurance Stocks: The Modern Gold Rush,* Arthur Milton wrote:

And many who work for the mutual companies actually think naïvely that they are in a non-profit service industry akin to education and public health! In other words, they think of themselves as dedicated professional men rather than grubbers for profits. In consequence, thousands of good life insurance salesmen, agents, and other personnel are abysmally ignorant of the vast profitability of their own industry.[1]

And *these* are the people inside the industry. The ignorance of the public is even more abysmal, for it is the public, in the form of the policyholder, who supplies this vast profitability. Those in the business—ignorant or not—are the recipients of it.

The mutual life insurance company is completely unique. In sheer economic size the companies stagger the imagination. The two largest, Prudential and Metropolitan, *each* has assets in excess of $23.5 *billion.* They are operated far more loosely than the stock companies. Their officers' salaries, sales commissions, and other expenses run much higher than those of stock companies. The reason for this is simple. The board of directors and officers of a stock company are answerable to the stockholders, and a sorry job is rewarded by loss of the job.

Mutual companies, on the other hand, are literally answerable to no one. The policyholders, ostensibly the "owners," are in fact completely without power insofar as the operation of the company is concerned. The power structure in a mutual company is self-perpetuating, the directors being picked by the officers, and the officers supposedly by the directors. The president of State Farm Mutual, quoted in an article in *Business Week,* summed it up by saying: "No one is going to fire me if I don't do a good job." [2]

The Armstrong investigation in the early part of this century recognized this same oddity in its report of 1906.

> It is of importance that officers should realize their direct responsibility to those whom they represent and should rely for their continuance in office upon proved efficiency and not upon a practical inability of the policyholders to depose them.[3]

No one—or, at least, not the men referred to—did anything about this condition, for more than 30 years later the Senate's Temporary National Economic Committee (TNEC) touched on the same subject in its conclusions: "Life insurance executives and directors constitute a small group that is self-appointing and self-perpetuating." [4]

Another 30 years-plus have passed since TNEC, and the situation remains the same, which proves, if nothing else, that self-perpetuation is not easy to stop.

Murray D. Lincoln while president of Nationwide Life Insurance Company was also on the board of directors of another large Midwestern mutual life insurance company. Lincoln told the president of the mutual company: "Society isn't going to let a few of you guys sit on top of three hundred and fifty million dollars and pass around the directorships to your friends and golf partners." [5]

But the guys sitting on top are not going to make it easy for society to push them off.

The Profitability of Nonprofit

In the curious upside-down world of life insurance, the policies available from a mutual company, which by any logic should cost less than the policies offered by an investor-profit-motivated stock company, actually require a premium of up to 30 percent *more* than the insurance available from the stock companies. This is called "participating" insurance, ostensibly because the owners of such policies will "participate" in the profits of the company. The policyholder is led to believe that he will receive "dividends" on his policy.

Here, again, we run into the arbitrary rewriting of the dictionary by the life insurance industry. A dividend received by the owner of a participating life insurance policy is not a dividend at all. It is a partial rebate of an overpayment.

A Certified Public Accountant, Albert Greenhouse, writing in *Finance* magazine, stated that

the word "dividend" as applied to a life insurance policy, is a misnomer and is, in fact, entirely misleading. An insurance dividend should never be considered a return on an investment, but rather a return of premiums paid.[6]

What is the point in collecting an excess premium with the intent of returning it? The fact is, it is an economic impossibility for a mutual company to return the entire overpayment, much less a profit on it. This overpayment, like the first overpayment that goes toward establishing the "savings" supposedly synonymous with Cash Surrender Value, is subject to the same drains of high salesman commissions, premium taxes (in most cases), and the expense of home office accounting.

In *A Study of Mutual Life Insurance Dividends,* Frank S. J. McIntosh pointed out a possible reason for the entire removal of the mutual companies from the economic scene. Wrote McIntosh:

> If the stock companies can make the tremendous profits of which they are accused by mutual company representatives, then this is the most damning evidence that the mutuals with their excessive premiums and excessive costs are either horribly mismanaged or that the mutual system, in itself, is so inefficient and antiquated that it should be removed from the present day economic scene.[7]

Stock companies are not the only ones that make tremendous profits. The mutuals are right in there with them, the difference being that instead of their profits going to the stockholders (the only *true* dividends in the life insurance business), they wind up in vast surpluses retained by the company.

However, the arguments over participating insurance are really nothing more than a decoy insofar as the individual buyer of life insurance is concerned. The mutual companies are not alone in offering this type of policy. Some stock companies combat the fallacious "dividend" offer not by refuting it, but by offering it along with their regular line of nonparticipating policies. Some do not.

Those who do not offer it use the difference in premium payments as their weapon against the mutuals. As an example of this, and the manner in which it takes the prospective buyer's eye off the principal issue of the need for *pure* death protection, was an ad one nonparticipating company ran under the heading, "WHERE IS THE OTHER $5,000?"

The case involved a man who had two friends in the life insurance business. One sold him a $25,000 nonparticipating policy, and the other sold him a $20,000 participating policy, both policies calling for approximately the same annual premium.

The policyholder died not long after taking the two policies out, and the two death-claim checks were delivered to the widow. Glancing at the $20,000 payment made on the participating policy, she asked, "Where is the other $5,000?"

Let's take the case a giant step further before we let the widow ask her embarrassing question. Let's suppose the man had a third friend in the life insurance business, a *true* friend who sold him pure death protection in the form of Decreasing Term to Age 65.

The age of the late lamented policyholder was not given, but let's say he was 35. The cheapest form of "permanent" insurance, whole or straight life, would have cost roughly $19.20 per $1,000 for nonparticipating, and $22.85 per $1,000 for participating, insurance. The annual premium, then, for the $25,000 nonparticipating policy (including waiver of premium and policy charge) would have been $480.00. The annual premium on the $20,000 participating would have been slightly lower—$457.00.

The one left out—the Decreasing Term to Age 65—would have cost only $3.74 per $1,000. Including the same waiver of premium and policy cost, the widow would have received *$120,000* for an annual premium of $470.56.

The question the widow asked should not have been "Where is the other $5,000?" It should have been "Where is the other $100,000?"

Law requires that mutual life insurance companies sell only "participating" insurance, and "participating" insurance requires a needless overcharge—even on pure term policies— in order that "dividends" (rebates) may be paid.

Therefore, do not—*under any circumstance*—consider buying your pure death protection from a mutual company.

Chapter 18

The "Net Cost" Farce

A life insurance salesman who feels that he is about to lose a client because of the high premium on a particular "permanent" policy will likely haul out pen and paper and, with a few deft strokes, perform a neat little trick called "net cost." This maneuver will *prove* to the prospect that the premium he will pay is not the cost of his insurance. It goes like this: A $10,000 "permanent" policy with an annual premium of $200 has been in force for 20 years. At the end of the 20-year period the Cash Surrender Value is $3,000. Has the insurance cost $200 a year? The salesman will smile benignly and shake his head. He will then jot down the following simple bit of arithmetic.

$200 times 20 years =	$4,000	Total premiums paid
	$3,000	Cash Surrender Value after 20 years
	———	
	$1,000	"Net cost" of insurance for 20 years
$1,000 divided by 20 years	= $50 per year	
$50 per year for $10,000 insurance	= $5 per $1,000	

Simple enough. But is it correct? *Better Homes and Gardens* magazine says it is:

> To figure the net cost of . . . a policy at the end of any given year, look up the cash value for that year and subtract it from the total amount of premiums paid by that time. Then

divide by the number of years and you have the average annual cost.[1]

If this "net cost" of life insurance is a factual presentation, it is just as reasonable for the would-be policyholder to smile back at the smiling salesman and say: "Fine. Then instead of paying your company the $200 annual premium, I'll just send a check for the $50 'net cost.' "

"Sorry," the salesman would answer. "We just can't do that."

The illustration just given applies to a nonparticipating policy, that is, a policy that does *not* pay the "dividends" (rebates) that were discussed in the previous chapter. The mutual life insurance companies—and the stock companies that offer participating policies—sweeten the pot even more by adding to it some fancy guesswork. By doing this, they can easily show a prospect that his insurance will cost him *nothing*, and go even further to show him he makes a profit. The "net cost" of a participating policy is figured in the following manner:

A $10,000 "permanent" policy, with an annual premium of $250, after 20 years would look something like this (as the salesman carries you imaginatively into the future):

$5,000	Total premiums paid (20 years times $250)
$3,000	Cash Surrender Value
$2,000	Difference between premiums paid and "savings" accumulated
$2,000	"Dividends" paid over 20-year period (*not* guaranteed, but "estimated")
0	"Net Cost" of insurance for 20 years

The big variable in this sort of "net costing" is, of course, the way the "dividend" is estimated. *Probe* came up with an interesting example of this. Under the heading "The Last Word" it reported that:

> One company inadvertently discovered that one of its agents had presented a prospect with a dividend illustration, the figures of which were 15% above the company's own liberal estimate. When they called the agent to task for jacking up the dividend projection he said, "What's wrong with what I did? You estimate dividends and feel that you're O.K. because you say clearly in the illustration, 'Dividends are estimates, not guaranteed.' Well, I did the very same thing in my illustration, too, only I think that, with reduced mortality, rise in interest rates, etc., dividends will be 15% higher during the next 20 years than you expect them to be. I've got just as much right to guess as you have, haven't I?" [2]

That is exactly what projected dividend estimates are—a guess. As such, they have no place whatever in a supposed "factual" presentation of the cost of a life insurance policy.

Happily, some industry executives are concerned about the misrepresentation in selling by this "net cost" method. Mr. Valentine Howell, a vice president and actuary of the Prudential Insurance Company, noted that the

> practice of showing net cost as the difference between the net payments and the cash surrender value, by the way, is a usual one in life insurance circles, in spite of its theoretical incorrectness and absurd results. By it, the "net cost" of endowment contracts can often be shown to be less than nothing. [3]

A vice president (now president) of Northwestern Mutual, Mr. Robert E. Dineen, in recalling remarks made by a fellow mutual company man, said:

> Mr. Gladstone Marshall, of the Connecticut Mutual, made a very scholarly presentation in which he said that by the use of the pencil you could produce any net cost picture you

wanted. Just by redistributing the figures, you could achieve any result. And the impression was that, in this respect, the actuaries were the captives of the sales department. In other words, whatever dividend was needed, could be generated.[4]

Some life insurance men, then, balk at the use of this tactic in doing business with the policy-buying public. However, this opposition has little or no effect on continuation of the practice. For example, Prudential, the company for which Mr. Howell worked, was still sponsoring the "net cost" practice across the country more than 20 years after Howell pointed out its "theoretical incorrectness and absurd results." Recently Prudential published this "net cost" example:

Illustration of a $100,000 Executive Whole Life Policy for Business Insurance Purposes

Male	Issue Age 40
$ 2,873.00	Annual Premium
$87,605.00	Total Cash—Age 65*
$15,780.00	Net Gain—Age 65[5]

*Includes cash value, accumulated dividends and termination dividends (based on 1964 scale, not guaranteed for future).

The footnote tells a part of the story. But let's examine the whole thing. The 40-year-old man paid an annual premium of $2,873.00 for 25 years—to age 65. The total premiums paid, then, would be $71,825.00.

Prudential neglects to tell us what proportion of the Total Cash of $87,605.00 is guaranteed Cash Surrender Value and what proportion is the guessed-at "dividends." However, even if the entire amount were guaranteed, which the footnote assures us is *not* the case, Prudential has seen fit to overlook one fairly sizable item—the *interest* that is being foregone on the premiums paid to the company. Mehr and Osler, in *Mod-*

ern Life Insurance, state that these "net cost illustrations elim-
inate the whole question of interest. If interest on premium
deposits were considered in net cost illustrations, the picture
would be entirely different." [6]

Let's look at Prudential's all-your-money-back-plus policy
in this light. According to a compound interest table, an investment of $1 a year for 25 years at a very modest 3 percent
interest will *not* be $25 at the end of the period. It will have
grown to $36.46. Therefore, the man who has paid Prudential
an annual premium of $2,873.00 over a 25-year period has
not relinquished only $71,825.00, or 25 times the annual pre-
mium. He has turned over to the company $71,825.00 *plus*
compound interest. Interest assumptions on an annual deposit
of $2,873.00 over 25 years are as follows for several rates:

Percent Interest	Total with Interest
3	$104,749.58
3.5	$111,903.25
4	$119,631.72
4.5	$128,020.88
5	$137,128.00

It would appear from this that Prudential and all the other
companies who use the "net cost" sales gimmick are, to say
the very least, not making full disclosure to the buyer of the
true cost of such insurance. The misconceptions resulting
from this type of sales presentation are not going entirely
unnoticed, however. *Forbes* magazine warned that the life
insurance industry could be in for a thorough going over by
the Federal Government. In an interview, Representative Benjamin S. Rosenthal (D) of New York, chairman of the House
Government Operations Committee's special consumer in-
quiry, was quoted as saying:

There isn't any question in my mind but that there should be full disclosure on *everything* a consumer buys, be it packages, bottles, loans, or insurance. The states haven't done a job on getting this information out in uniform manner. It should be the Federal Government's responsibility.[7]

"Net costing" life insurance in the manner that it is done is not full disclosure. In fact, it is nothing less than a distortion of the true cost of the product. Let's take the example given at the start of this chapter, a $10,000 "permanent" policy, with an annual premium of $200, and at the end of 20 years a Cash Surrender Value of $3,000.

$4,000   Total premiums paid over 20-year period
$1,467   Compound interest at 4% *lost* by policyholder on the annual average increase of $150 on the Cash Surrender Value for 20 years
_____

$5,467   Total cost for 20 years

Now, if the policyholder, at the end of the 20-year period, chooses to cash in, or "junk," his policy, he will receive the $3,000 Cash Surrender Value. Subtracting this from the total cost, we find that the "Net Cost" was $2,467, *not* $1,000 as the salesman's "net cost" pitch would lead us to believe.

The same principle applies to "participating" policies, except that the rebates, or "dividends," should be omitted for the simple reason that they can only be estimated, and, as we have seen, they can be juggled to make "net cost" appear to be anything the salesman thinks will expedite the sale of the policy.

The president of Minnesota Mutual, Mr. Harold J. Cummings, must have given the American Life Convention a shock in 1957 when he said in a speech:

We may as well be blunt about it . . . any prospective customer must conclude that net-cost comparisons, however plausible, are inconclusive if not misleading, ill-advised if not fictitious, deceptive if not deceitful, asinine if not downright dishonest.[8]

Chapter 19

Stock Companies—The Astronauts of the Investment World

"With some 60% of the life insurance business done by the mutuals who feature the 'no profit theme,' the stock companies are content to 'ride along under this umbrella' and avoid spotlighting the profitability of the life insurance business."

—Dart Publications

While the mutual and stock companies in the life insurance industry compete with each other in the selling of their product, each needs the other to continue doing business. Particularly do the stock companies need the mutual companies. If their enormous profits are ever questioned, they can say: "We are competing successfully against mutual companies which are 'nonprofit,' so how can we be accused of making a killing on what we sell when the public can buy its life insurance at 'cost' from the mutual companies?"

The answer is, of course, that nonprofitability is one trait that cannot be attributed to either the stock or the mutual companies. The profits are there, and they are of a magnitude that strains belief.

Some investors were aware of the tremendous profitability of life insurance shares prior to the late 1950s. If there was one single thing that spread this awareness far and wide, it was an article that appeared in the December 15, 1959, issue of *Forbes* magazine. The lead into the article asked: "You're probably heard that many smart millionaires have been attracted to the life insurance business. But do you know why?"

The article featured the Franklin Life Insurance Company, of Springfield, Illinois, and the company's chief executive, Charles E. Becker. Becker and his associates bought control of Franklin Life in 1939 for approximately $1 million. By the end of 1959 the original investment had grown to more than $85 million, *Forbes* reported.

This 8,400 percent appreciation in two decades on Franklin stock could hardly go unnoticed. In explaining the success of the company, Becker credited it in part to "the high-premium policies in which we specialize. . . . I can afford to pay our agents top commissions and still generate high profits for our stockholders."

Lately the Securities and Exchange Commission has taken a dim view of securities salesmen who make 7 to 8.5 percent on the sale of investment trust shares. The SEC wants to cut it to 5 percent.

What about Franklin's salesmen? Under the heading "Cutting the Premium Pie," a slice labeled 14 percent went to agents' commissions. Of course, the SEC has no jurisdiction over this, nor does any other agency. This means that such sales commissions, exorbitant as they may be, are legal unless or until effective controls of one form or another are established.

The *Forbes* article offered nothing new to those who had already become millionaires from ownership of life insurance stock. In fact, many of them did not care for the spotlight being focused on a relatively unknown gold mine. But the attention was focused, and from 1960 through 1964 the life stocks were off and running. The performances of life companies were nothing short of astounding in the 13-year period from 1951 to 1964. The following chart shows the results of a $10,000 investment in several stock life insurance companies, including cash dividends paid and increase in value of shares:

Table No. 6 [1]

	1951	1964
1. Philadelphia Life	$10,000	$1,122,285.85
2. Franklin Life	$10,000	484,769.18
3. United States Life	$10,000	409,753.06
4. Commonwealth Life (Ky.)	$10,000	347,763.87
5. Liberty National Life	$10,000	271,728.21
6. Bankers National Life	$10,000	255,937.13
7. Southland Life	$10,000	250,268.56
8. Kansas City Life	$10,000	186,624.00
9. West Coast Life	$10,000	169,505.32
10. Gulf Life	$10,000	162,833.75
11. National Life and Accident	$10,000	152,328.50
12. Southwestern Life	$10,000	129,363.69
13. Connecticut General Life	$10,000	126,857.08
14. Jefferson Standard Life	$10,000	116,889.77
15. Lincoln National Life	$10,000	112,090.67
16. Aetna Life	$10,000	104,124.60
17 Travelers Insurance	$10,000	102,082.01
18. Life of Virginia	$10,000	74,206.83

While some stocks leveled or dropped off from this 1964 peak, the boom was by no means over. A "swap fund" in the spring of 1966 reported that $8,150,857 worth of life insurance stocks had been deposited with the company.[2] The original cost of those stocks had been $633,770. Several issues listed were: Jefferson Standard Life, showing a market value of $1,410,395 and a cost of $30,597; Lincoln National, with a value of $1,160,880 and a cost of $56,007; National Life and Accident, with a value of $435,487 and a cost of $36,974.

With the irony that at times seems built into the life insurance industry, this vast profitability became a source of alarm to some life insurance men. Halsey Josephson, an editor of *Probe,* penned an article for the January 10, 1966, issue that is in itself alarming, at least to the owner of life insurance policies. Under the heading, "Profit Is a Risky Word," Josephson wrote:

> The nomenclature of the life insurance business seems to attract visitors who become permanent guests. Up to a year or two ago, our favorites (because they had built-in deception)* were "refinements" and "innovations." Now it has become fashionable to speak of "profit" and "profitability." We submit that they are dangerous additions to our vocabulary.
>
> To most people, profit means "the excess of the price received over the cost of purchasing and handling, or of producing and marketing particular goods." In a mutual company, profit, in this sense, is theoretically nonexistent. And in an established stock company, it has extremely limited significance. In the latter, investors expect and receive only a modest return on their investment. We know that if stock companies charged a material excess over the cost of "producing and marketing" it would be non-competitive with the mutuals, and the return to investors would disappear entirely. . . .
>
> What profitability then are we talking about? And who gets it? True, we aim to sell at adequate rates, and we must establish margins of safety, and we must maintain legitimate reserves. But these are not profits in the business sense. Whatever they are, the public has long since accepted the legitimacy, and even necessity, for them. But "profit" carries an entirely different connotation, and a dangerous one.
>
> Should the public come to believe—and it may—if we continue to use such ill-advised words that life insurance companies are managed like manufacturing concerns and have

* The parenthetical phrase is not ours; it is *Probe*'s.

the same economic motivations, it will be alienated and we will be headed for trouble.

Probe wonders what profitability they were talking about, and who received the profit. Apparently the editors did not recall another editorial they published little more than a year earlier, in the November 16, 1964, issue, entitled: "Trouble Ahead":

> Perhaps up to now the investing public and the non-investing reading public have not related the fantastic growth of new life insurance company stock to the cost of their personal life insurance. But that relationship will, in time, occur to millions. What makes the value of any common stock rise? The public will quite naturally assume that they stem directly from the margin between the actual cost of insurance and the premiums charged. And when life insurance stock is so certain to rise in predictable leaps and bounds, that margin, many people will ultimately come to believe, is excessive. And when people start to believe that, the life insurance business, including established as well as new companies, will be in trouble.

It is not the purpose of this book to take issue with the necessity of profits in a society such as ours. However, the life insurance industry occupies an unusual position, that of providing what has long since come to be recognized as a necessity. The excessive and hidden profits made by it are reflected directly in what many life insurance men consider to be the "woefully underinsured" American public.

One stock company executive, Mr. W. D. Grant, president of Business Men's Assurance, of Kansas City, Missouri, speaking at the 1966 American Life Convention in Denver, revealed the results of a survey conducted at his behest. Picking 30 names at random from an obituary column, Grant had inquiries made as to the income and life insurance of these individuals.

"Incredible as it seems," said Grant, "only one individual owned as much as $17,500 of life insurance." [3] He found the average to be $8,427. Two had no life insurance whatever, and one had a mere $500.

Mr. Grant, whose stock holdings in Business Men's Assurance had a market value in 1967 of $9.8 million, apparently found this underinsured state of the public at large to be startling. However, if the industry—including Mr. Grant's own company—would make pure death protection more readily available to the public, this condition of "woeful underinsurance" could very readily be reversed.

Chapter 20

G.I. Insurance and the Military Market

"Whatever sympathetic interest we may feel for the defenders of our country in time of war, as a business proposition they are not worth any special effort to secure their patronage."
— Richard McCurdy, President of Mutual Life of New York (MONY), 1885–1906

There are two important "don'ts" for any veteran fortunate enough to have his National Service Life Insurance in force and in its original form of pure term insurance: (1) don't drop it, and (2) don't let anyone—and that includes the Veterans Administration itself, talk you into converting it to a "permanent" plan.

G.I. insurance (term), especially policies issued prior to 1951, is the best bargain there has ever been in life insurance. The cost is lower than any insurance available through private companies because administration costs are not borne by the policyholders, but come from general expense funds of the government.

The life insurance industry has sulked about National Service Life Insurance ever since, through its own thumb-twiddling, it forced the government into the life insurance business. Since World War II powerful lobbying efforts have been made to block the reinstatement of National Service Life Insurance for those veterans who let their coverage lapse. This inexpensive term insurance has apparently caused many veterans to wonder about the "advantages" of the high-priced "permanent" policies life companies push.

The industry has found a powerful ally, however, in trying to create suspicion about term insurance. The Veterans Administration sends out "permanent" propaganda along with the premium notices to veterans. A premium notice (VA Form 29-483, January, 1966) contains several warnings about the evils that supposedly lurk in the term policy. "Premiums will continue to increase at older ages," says the Veterans Administration. "The sooner you convert the lower the premium," and "While term insurance has its uses, it is not designed for lifetime protection. The increase in premiums required can be burdensome, if not prohibitive, in the later stages of life."

Sounds a little like the old company line? There's more. An enclosure entitled "GI Insurance Fact: Should You Convert Your GI Term Policy to a Permanent Plan?" features a cartoon depicting three old soldiers driving little cars across the page. The Veterans Administration's answer to its own question is plain enough. One driver, labeled "20 Pay," rides smoothly out to age 60 and stops. A second, "Ordinary Life," is still cruising happily at between age 80 and 85, seemingly in great shape and hell-bent on making it to 100, paying his premiums all the way. "Term," meanwhile, is having a rough go of it in the third car. At age 70, sweating, hat askew, the car radiator boiling over, this veteran is in dire straits because of old Prohibitive Cost.

It is the same "permanent" Cash Surrender Value line parroted millions of times every day by life insurance salesmen from coast to coast. As usual, there is no mention that the higher premium the others pay for their "permanent" plans has simply been advance payment for the very time the "term" veteran is supposedly finding it too difficult to go on. Nor is it mentioned that the excess premiums going into the Cash Surrender Value "savings" account are steadily allowing the death protection in the policies to drop, and that this Cash Surrender Value, like that in company-issued policies, will disappear at the time the veteran dies. The actual fact is that all three veterans (even the "20 Pay") are all paying relatively the same cost per $1,000 rate—the rate that the "huffing and puffing" term veteran is paying. They just don't know it.

This "conversion" propaganda distributed by the Veterans Administration is good news to the life insurance industry. The *National Underwriter* referred to one such sally as a "splendid boost":

> Perhaps it's because we're in the middle of "Brotherhood Week," but a few days ago the concept of the preferability of permanent life insurance over term coverage received a splendid boost from a rather unexpected source—the federal government.[1]

A great many life insurance salesmen have not been satisfied with simply having the preferability of "permanent" drummed into the heads of these veterans, and have actively "twisted" these invaluable policies and replaced them with commission-producing "permanent" policies. The *National Underwriter* wagged an editorial finger at the bad record such tactics were making for the industry, but wound up on a note that seemed to indicate a curious double standard of ethics for life insurance salesmen: "Admittedly National Service Life Insurance is a tempting target for agents. In many respects it seems less reprehensible to twist NSLI than to twist business from another company." [2]

The sale of the original National Service Life Insurance was halted in 1951 and a new policy was introduced during the Korean conflict. This was basically the same, but with one important watered-down feature which, while not totally appeasing the life insurance industry, was a slight improvement from its point of view. The new policy did not have the dividend provision, though it still allowed veterans to continue the coverage as term insurance after separation from the service.

This form of National Service Life Insurance was halted as of December 31, 1956.

The men fighting in Vietnam had the misfortune of being up against an older and wiser life insurance industry. While lobbying continued against the reintroduction of National Service Life Insurance, many of the individual companies did not care to insure such men. In October, 1965, *Business Week* reported that Prudential had announced in May, 1965, it would no longer write policies for servicemen headed for Vietnam. The magazine went on to say that much of the industry "fell in behind Mother Pru." [3]

The inevitable result of this abandonment of servicemen was that during the summer of 1965 efforts were begun in Congress to give them $10,000 free life insurance. The industry immediately announced its opposition to the proposal. Life insurance salesmen, through their National Association of Life Underwriters (NALU), called the plan "a needless and unwarranted intrusion by the federal government into a market which can and should be served by the private insurance business." [4] Even though such powerful lobbies as the Veterans of Foreign Wars and the Disabled American Veterans were strongly in favor of the bill, the life insurance industry won out.

In the bill that was passed, private companies were to underwrite servicemen's life insurance under a group policy. The life insurance industry called the tune. The $10,000 policy offered was to cost service personnel $2 a month, paid by allotment. At the option of the individual, he or she could take the full $10,000, $5,000 (at $1 a month), or none. Prudential was named as "prime contractor," with more than 500 companies to share in the underwriting.

The catch for the G.I.—and the great appeal to the life insurance industry—is that the Servicemen's Group Life Insurance, unlike the original National Service Life Insurance coverage, cannot be continued in civilian life as term insurance. There is a 120-day period of "free" coverage after separation from the service, but to continue any insurance past this period without evidence of insurability it is mandatory that the ex-serviceman *convert to a form of permanent insurance with one of the participating companies.*

This forces G.I.'s who have suffered service-connected disabilities that make them uninsurable to carry this insurance with a private, profit-making concern. At the same time the Servicemen's Group Life Insurance guarantees some life insurance salesman who had absolutely nothing to do with the original purchase a nice first-year commission, as well as automatic renewal commissions for as long as the ex-G.I. lives or is able to pay the premiums. This is a sort of bonus-in-reverse, which the veterans pay to the salesmen.

There is even a built-in guarantee that the casualties of war will not interfere with their profit, since the life companies will pay only the normal mortality costs, and, as the *National Underwriter* pointed out, "The government absorbs above-average mortality costs due to combat and other causes." [5] The government, as you may recall, is run by tax dollars.

What does this mean? Simply that the life insurance companies were handed the biggest group plum in history, that their profit was guaranteed, and all survivors of the group were automatic prospects for forced "conversion" to "permanent" insurance after being separated from the service. The losers are the servicemen, who will be compelled to convert, and the general public, which has been included as co-insurer on all death claims "due to combat or other causes."

The Serviceman as an Individual Target

Mail-order life insurance companies appealing to servicemen and their families have become a major problem. The March, 1967, issue of *Consumer Reports* magazine noted:

John R. Reilly, Federal Trade Commission member, recently warned of "what appears to be cynically deceptive marketing practices" by mail-order insurance companies. Life insurance policies arrive in the mail already made out to relatives of recently inducted men, he said, and these policies are "designed to appear identical to the well-known $10,000 life insurance policies covering American veterans. . . .

"According to the allegations I have seen, the solicited consumer is also deceived as to policy coverage, premiums payable, pre-existing conditions, statistics—the works! The situation is bad and becoming worse with time. The American consumer should not have to live with it." [6]

A vice president of one Arizona-based life insurance company was tried and convicted in Federal court of bribery for having paid an Air Force sergeant $27,000 over an 18-month period merely to supply the names of new recruits and the addresses of their parents. Apparently the mail solicitation business was sufficiently lucrative to justify the payment of such a commission. [7]

Some life insurance salesmen track down the rookies in a legal manner. Mr. Seymour Petrovsky, of Business Men's Assurance, advising his fellow salesmen in a trade journal, revealed that he got his prospects by keeping an eye on the military news of his home-town paper. He did not move in immediately because "I knew that . . . would lead only to bumping into every new life insurance salesman in the city." So he waited eight weeks until basic training was over and the boys were coming home on furlough. He then would call the parents of the boys and introduce himself, saying, "I represent my company as their government insurance representative," and would attempt to set up an appointment.

Where is the money in selling life insurance to young men in uniform? Petrovsky went on to explain: "Usually if the parent can understand what I am trying to get across, an interview is the result. I offer only one plan to these men—30-pay life." [8]

A young man—whether in the military service of his country or not—needs a high-priced 30-pay life insurance policy about as much as a catfish needs feathers. Why should these young men be offered *only* one policy? Why should they be denied the choice of buying a term policy? They are required to pay, in a very real sense, for the privilege of serving in the armed forces.

The Foreign Legion

Join the life insurance business and see the world. Service personnel are no longer able to escape life insurance salesmen by going overseas. The industry has its own band of camp followers, and if the enticements offered these foreign agents are any indication, business is booming. Companies approved by the Defense Department for operation on overseas American bases lure salesmen with such things as "far less competition than in the states"; "a lower cost of living"; "116% first year commission"; and "domestic help is cheaper."

The market consists of military personnel and their dependents, and it is all neatly rounded up by Uncle Sam with periodic rotation of personnel to supply an automatic stream of new prospects.

Conclusions

If you have National Service Life Insurance, keep it, and keep it as term insurance. The ancient argument that the cost is prohibitive at older ages is equally true of *any* life insurance policy.

The veteran who has been covered under Servicemen's Group Life Insurance can thank the life insurance industry for being denied the opportunity of continuing this as pure death protection, or term insurance, after separation from the service. When the salesmen come around, point this out to them. Then, if there exists a need for life insurance, tell them to forget about "converting" and to get out the rate book on Decreasing Term to Age 65.

Chapter 21

Industrial and Credit Life Insurance

"As long as men will be compelled to prostitute their honor, and as long as reward and promotion are offered those capable of lying most, so long must this graft continue."
—*Confessions of an Industrial Insurance Agent*

Industrial insurance is a lingering example of the overeager marketing habits of the industry. The beginnings of this type of insurance occurred during the industrial revolution, at a time when workers' wages were notoriously low. Factory workers were unable to buy life insurance in more than token amounts, usually intended simply as a burial fund. In fact, morticians sold industrial insurance and found it unusually profitable because it enabled them to collect the premiums during the policyholder's lifetime and the death benefit when he died.

The face amount ranged downward from $1,000 and the premiums were collected weekly, generally on payday at the worker's home before he could spend the money elsewhere. The conditions that spawned industrial insurance have virtually disappeared. Social Security, group insurance, and a better-paid and somewhat better-informed public have all resulted in a steady decline in the amount of industrial insurance in force. Even so, almost half the current individual policies in existence in the United States are for industrial insurance.

The market still consists of people of low income, many of whom are illiterate and who have a limited concept of what

143

life insurance is all about. The disadvantages these people encounter at the hands of the salesman—or "debit man," as he is called—are multiplied by the pressure exerted on the salesman by the companies to put new insurance on the books. This results in a great deal of ill-advised coverage, such as policies on wives and children which would be better placed on the father, and in an extremely high lapse rate.

Industrial rates are the highest in the whole field of life insurance. Companies attempt to justify this by pointing out the high cost of making weekly collection of premiums, yet the high lapse rate more than offsets this cost. Industrial insurance, unlike other forms of "permanent" insurance, does not have any Cash Surrender Value until the fifth year it is in force. This is stipulated by law, but competition may vary it. Thus policies that are lapsed during the first four years are, in effect, extremely expensive term insurance.

Of course, term insurance is just as good for a poor man as for the more fortunate. But the fear of widespread buying of reasonably priced term insurance permeates the industry. Twenty-five years ago an insurance text noted an alarming trend in the offing—a trend which, incidentally, never materialized:

> Some critics have suggested that only temporary term protection should be offered by the industrial companies; this suggestion poses as serious a challenge for the system as any which has been leveled at it.[1]

True to form, the great concern is for perpetuating the "system," not the welfare or real need of the insurance-buying public.

The persistence of such anachronisms as industrial insurance is one more sign of the inability of the present system of state regulation to cope with life insurance abuses.

Credit Life Insurance

Although the sale of industrial insurance appears to be on the wane, the exploitation of consumer-borrowers is on the upswing. Credit life insurance is used to repay a loan if the borrower dies. The idea is reasonable enough, but the way it actually works in many cases is not. Finance companies, in particular, load high-priced life insurance on top of their other high prices, and come out with additional millions in profit.

Approximately 80 percent of all consumer loans are covered by credit life insurance, with the premium rates based on each $100 of the loan. The rate varies from 37½ cents to $2 and more. An actuarial study reported by the Insurance Commissioner of Vermont showed that the cost of a claim was 30 cents per $100, with an administrative cost to the companies of less than 5 cents, which should certainly bring up some question about the higher rates charged.

The explanation is simple. The interests of the finance companies and the insurance companies are on the same side. Relatively few deaths occur among those insured under credit life. *New Republic* magazine reported that one company specializing in credit life took in $62.6 million in premiums in 1965, and paid out death benefits of $24.3 million, for a nice gross profit of 63 percent.

An assistant counsel for the Senate Antitrust and Monopoly Committee, Dean Sharp, said that an unpublished committee report on credit life insurance indicated that borrowers had been overcharged $700 million between 1959 and 1965.[2] As the volume increases every year, so does the overcharge. In 1966 it was estimated at $175 million.

Commissions are paid to the finance companies on the insurance sold, and in many cases year-end rebates are made from excess premium payments. In the trade they prefer to call this "retrospective rate credit." Of course, the process stops before it reaches the man who paid for it—the consumer-borrower.

In the September 5, 1967, issue of the *Wall Street Journal* it was reported that the Senate Antitrust Subcommittee was getting set to take a look into the pricing of credit life insurance. The report indicated that some of those possibly involved in this overcharge of the public might prefer to spread the light of government scrutiny over a wider area of the industry. Reported the *Journal*:

> Several finance company executives are known to feel that abuses are far greater in the sale of regular life insurance, and they will probably testify to this effect. The testimony could open up the whole area for future investigation.

The California insurance department, generally recognized as being on a par with that of New York, tried to lower the maximum rate on credit life insurance from 75 cents per $100 of indebtedness to a maximum of 65 cents, ranging down to 45 cents, depending upon the amount of indebtedness. The ruling, which was to go into effect in January, 1968, was nullified by a bill passed in the California legislature and signed into law by Governor Ronald Reagan.

The lack of meaningful regulation allows the abuses of credit life insurance—as well as all other areas of the industry —to continue unchecked.

Chapter 22

Social Security

"And social security, unlike actuarially funded insurance, is untouched by inflation: after Germany's terrible 1923 inflation, private insurance was wiped out but social insurance started all over as if nothing had happened."   —Paul A. Samuelson

When Social Security appeared on the American scene during Franklin Roosevelt's first term as President, the attack upon it was led by the life insurance industry. It was vilified as being, among other things, a step toward the end of the free enterprise system. Yet the life insurance industry itself played a considerable role in creating the conditions that spawned the Social Security Act. Dr. J. Owen Stalson, one of the most authoritative historians of life insurance, laid part of the blame at the industry's doorstep. In *Marketing Life Insurance* Stalson wrote:

> The companies continue to frown upon the sale of long term term; the public continues to hunger for low outlay, low cost, long term bare protection contracts. . . . Furthermore, failure on the part of the industry to meet this strong and long-standing demand has no doubt helped to produce the Social Security Act, which calls for a program looking toward long term, low rate, low cost term insurance through government action.[1]

The Social Security Act was passed in 1935. Payroll deductions began January 1, 1937. At this point it was primarily an old age pension plan, but in 1939 the life insurance aspect came into being in the form of "survivors' benefits." Some critics claim that Social Security is not life insur-

147

ance, but the fact that it pays a small lump sum in cash at death, and provides a predetermined schedule of monthly payments to a widow with dependent children, brings it well within the definition of life insurance. The fact that it is multipurpose does not mean that its components cannot be considered separately for what they are.

The notions that Social Security is an American invention and that we require more money to be paid for it than other countries are both wrong. The Elizabethan Poor Law was enacted in England in 1601, and even that was not the first such legislation. A recent study by the Brookings Institution showed that the United States ranked *twenty-first* among 22 major countries in Social Security expenditures as a percentage of national income.

The expenditures, along with the tax (premium), have risen periodically since the beginning. W. D. Grant, president of Business Men's Assurance Company, wrote in an article in a Retail Credit Company publication in September, 1967:

> While we have been emphasizing larger sales and accelerating our marketing efforts in the higher income groups, the Federal Government has not been overlooking the middle and lower income people. Quite the contrary, Social Security benefits have been extended dramatically and just how much may surprise you. Think of this—a man, age 30, with three children, ages 5, 3, and 1 and earning $6,600 a year, has Social Security coverage offering death benefits of $56,745. In 1950, the amount in similar circumstances was $35,651.[2]

Almost a third of a century after the beginning of the Social Security program, the life insurance industry seems strangely content to let the Federal Government look after the middle- and lower-income groups, while it continues to direct its sales efforts toward more affluent segments of the population.

Social Security, just like group or association insurance, should definitely be considered as part of a man's life insurance program. Yet, because of gaps in it—primarily the fact that the Social Security survivor payments stop when the last dependent child reaches the age of 18, or 22 if "under roof" and in school, and do not resume until the widow reaches age 62—it cannot take the place of privately purchased, pure death protection. It can only be considered a supplement to that necessary protection.

Social Security is apparently here to stay. The only effort the life insurance industry has made to serve the needs of the lower-income class is through industrial life insurance. If the industry had supplied the long-term, low-cost, death protection so sorely needed, the "survivors' benefits," or life insurance, aspect of Social Security might have been avoided. Because it failed to do so, governmental action became necessary.

Chapter 23

The Specialty Market

"The only thing advanced about advanced underwriting is getting to the prospect in advance of the other agent."
—A Life Insurance Company Vice President

While the run-of-the-mill life insurance salesman does his cold canvassing, there is an elite corps that goes strictly after important prospects. Here, in the rarefied atmosphere of the affluent, is the man in the Internal Revenue Service's upper tax bracket, and, even more than the little fellow, he always has an eye out for a tax break. The life insurance salesman is ready to accommodate him.

Minimum-Deposit Insurance

Some years ago the industry became alarmed at an upsurge in the sale of term insurance to people of means. The trend, if allowed to continue, would have cut badly into commission dollars. Accordingly, some new plan had to be formulated that would permit the sale of "permanent" Cash Surrender Value insurance as an apparent competitor to term. The result was "bank loan," or "minimum-deposit," insurance.

"Minimum-deposit" had an immediate attraction for people in high tax brackets. This is how it works:

The initial difference between the special minimum-deposit policy and other "permanent" types is that it contains a guaranteed first-year Cash Surrender Value, and this is substantial—up to 70 percent of the annual premium. As an example, suppose Dr. Brown, whose practice puts him in the over-50 percent tax bracket, is sold a minimum-deposit policy that calls for a $1,000 annual premium. The guaranteed Cash Surrender Value the first year is $700. Dr. Brown pays $300 cash and borrows the $700 from the company (the loans were made as bank loans in the days of low bank rates).

The second premium is made in the same manner, with Dr. Brown paying in cash the difference between the new Cash Surrender Value and the total premium. He now has interest to be paid to the life insurance company (or the bank) on the loan against the Cash Surrender Value. However, being in a high tax bracket, the interest can be deducted from his gross income, thus lowering the net rate substantially. If, for instance, his tax bracket is 50 percent, an interest rate of 5 percent will become a *net* rate of 2.5 percent.

With artificially high Cash Surrender Value accumulations, the premium—in the form of cash needed to meet it—may disappear entirely, leaving only the interest on the increasing loan to be paid. The scheme thus appears to be truly something-for-nothing. But money does not appear from nowhere, and someone is paying. Who?

Let's take a closer look at the first year's premium. The guaranteed Cash Surrender Value was $700, or 70 percent of the $1,000 premium. Yet Dr. Brown paid only $300, and the simplest arithmetic shows that $700 cannot be gotten out of $300. Nor can the cost of putting the policy on the company books. Nor can the salesman's commission, which itself will be more than the $300 cash paid.

Where does the money come from? If you happen to be a policyholder in the same company, *you* are paying it. The first-year Cash Surrender Value of $700 is acquired by siphoning it off from surpluses supplied by the premiums of old policyholders. The mutual companies excel at this. From their vast reserves and surpluses they not only create a first-year Cash Surrender Value, but also first-year "dividends" to sweeten the pot. One well-known actuary put it succinctly when he stated that there could not possibly be anything to borrow that had never been paid in or earned on the policy.

Other life insurance men felt uneasy about this on the grounds of unsound economics and possible intervention by the Internal Revenue Service on the tax loophole it afforded the wealthy buyer. It proved to be a very tough loophole to plug, as the Internal Revenue Service discovered, for if the right to deduct interest on such policy loans were denied the affluent policyholder interested only in the tax dodge, how could the little man be given the deduction, even if desperation drove him to taking out the loan?

Minimum-deposit insurance has several drawbacks not to be found in the purchase of pure death protection, or term, insurance. Several assumptions must be made in order to show minimum-deposit in a favorable light, and none of them can be guaranteed: (1) that the individual will continue to be in a high tax bracket; (2) that the present tax laws regarding interest will prevail; (3) that the guesses at the future "dividend" (rebate) rate will be reasonably accurate.

The waiver-of-premium clause, in event of disability after the loan against the policy had become considerable, would apply only to each year's premiums, and *not* to the interest that would have to be paid each year.

Finally, a point of no return arrives at which the interest cost on the steadily increasing loan becomes higher than the actual cost of the remaining death protection (the face amount of the policy *less* the borrowed Cash Surrender Value).

At this point there is nothing to do but drop the policy and pay off the loan with the Cash Surrender Value.

Split-Dollar Insurance

Split-dollar insurance, if it has done nothing else, has given its purchasers the opportunity of seeing that Cash Surrender Value allows the life insurance company to come steadily "off the risk." It has also come dangerously close to upsetting the business of the so-called "inside interest build-up" on Cash Surrender Values.

Split-dollar is a plan under which an employer can buy a "permanent" policy on a valuable employee, the employer paying in the "savings" or Cash Surrender Value portion of the premium, and the employee paying the portion applicable to the death protection in the policy. As a rule, the employer will pay the first year's premium, and, just as with minimum-deposit, the life insurance company digs into the surplus and pulls out a quick Cash Surrender Value, and possibly an even quicker dividend.

The employer, who each year thereafter puts up the exact amount that the Cash Surrender Value is to increase, has the Cash Surrender Value assigned to him in the event of the employee's death. The difference between this and the face amount of the policy (which is the amount the insurance company is "on the risk") goes to the employee's beneficiaries.

The advantage to the employer is that he can recoup the total amount put into the policy, whether termination is by death or by the employee moving on to another company and the policy lapsing.

The premium paid by the employee on his decreasing death protection declines (seemingly in direct opposition to the actuarial fact of increasing mortality costs with age) until—generally after the eighth year—no more premiums are paid by the employee. No, a miracle has not transpired. By foregoing the "inside interest build-up" on the rising Cash Surrender Value, this interest actually pays for the death protection remaining. The employer thus gives the employee a tax-free fringe benefit of death protection.

This, of course, was the idea from the beginning. Here was another something-for-nothing plan with a tax angle, and it did not take long to reach the sensitive nostrils of the Internal Revenue Service.

If this valuable employee had a substantial amount of death protection, and the proceeds were paid to his beneficiaries upon his death, then the premium for this death protection should legitimately be considered a part of his taxable income. Since no cash was being paid by the employer (or the employee, for that matter), the life insurance industry suddenly found the Internal Revenue Service looking squarely down its throat at the so-called "inside interest build-up" on the Cash Surrender Value. This imputed interest was now almost out in the open, and was dangerously close to being declared income.

Mr. Eugene Thoré, vice president and general counsel of the Life Insurance Association of America (LIAA), was once more hurried in to explain things to the Internal Revenue Service. The industry breathed a long sigh when the Service announced that the interest would not be taxed, but that the employee receiving the tax-sheltered insurance would be "held taxable annually in an amount equal to the one-year term cost of the declining life insurance protection to which the employee is entitled under such an arrangement, less any portion of the premium provided by him."

The *National Underwriter* reported a speech made by Mr. Thoré in which he pointed out why this approach by the Internal Revenue Service was so valuable to the life insurance industry: "Unlike the interest approach, it would not come dangerously close to creating a precedent for taxing the so-called interest build-up." [1]

Key-Man Insurance

This differs basically from "split-dollar" in that the policy taken out on a key man, whose death would be financially injurious to the company, is paid for by the employer and the employer is the beneficiary. This coverage has a very practical place, because in the case of the loss of such a man, his future economic value could be replaced to the employer.

However, much of this is sold in the form of "permanent" Cash Surrender Value insurance.

"Minimum-deposit," "split-dollar," "key-man," and any other plan of "permanent" life insurance offered by the industry has as its prime purpose the acquisition of the premium money that represents the difference between the cost of pure death protection and the garbled Cash Surrender Value "savings" or "investment." The same general rule applies to these variations as to the average man protecting his family through life insurance. If you need life insurance, buy the pure thing—term.

Chapter 24

Propaganda

"The only value in finding out what the public wants, should it differ from what we want, is to help us in preparing material to swing them around to our way of thinking." —*Probe*

Like any other major industry, the life insurance companies are very much concerned with the industry's image. For this reason, the various companies' annual advertising outlay of more than $50 million is aimed not directly at the sale of life insurance, but at providing a proper "image" and building a favorable and friendly aura about the field men. A vice president of the Institute of Life Insurance, speaking of its TV advertising budget of $2 million, said: "Even if the public ignored our messages . . . their galvanizing effect on 250,000 [full-time] volatile, highly charged agents has been worth the cost." [1]

The $2 million that the Institute puts into TV ads comes from the companies that support it, and the money the companies turn over to the Institute comes from the policyholders. Next time you mail a premium off to some home office, consider that somewhere in that check is money that will be spent "galvanizing" a quarter of a million life insurance salesmen. Gives you a lump in the throat, doesn't it?

The Prudential has been a long-time believer in the effectiveness of television as an advertising medium. "What people think of us as guarantors of their security is very important," said a Prudential executive, "and, therefore, our whole TV effort—the program itself as well as the commercial—is aimed at building an image of a company that is strong and progressive and operated in the public interest." [2]

While television gets the lion's share of the life insurance advertising dollar, the high-circulation magazines don't come off badly, as anyone knows who has ever opened a copy of *Life, Look, Reader's Digest, Better Homes and Gardens,* etc.

A few—Allstate, for example—advocate particular policies. Others push the "image" and "professionalism." Mutual of New York (MONY) starts off with opposition from the prospect ("Look, I work for a helicopter company. I'd rather invest in that than buy life insurance!") and winds up with its professional straightening everything out—by laying some "permanent" Cash Surrender Value life insurance on the prospect. This makes the prospect grateful. ("The special help Arthur and MONY gave me is just amazing!")

Others pursue a pseudo-religious approach. Massachusetts Mutual, just before Easter, runs a Norman Rockwell sketch showing Mom, Dad, and the two kids kneeling in a church pew. (But Massachusetts Mutual isn't selling religion, it's selling "permanent" life insurance.)

The "Facts" of Life Insurance

Everyone knows, of course, that the ultimate purpose of advertising is to sell something. So, while this sort of propaganda comes in by the front door, another kind walks in the back. Advertising paraded under the banner of unbiased journalism is nothing new to the life insurance industry. Way back in 1844, Mutual of New York had an entry in its accounts which read: "Paid to Editor of Ev. Post for inserting an article on life insurance, $10.00." [3]

Today, articles about life insurance appear in professional journals, newsletters, magazines, and newspapers all over the country. Almost without exception, these speak out in favor of "permanent" Cash Surrender Value life insurance. Writers of columns on etiquette as well as financial writers (who should, and maybe *do,* know better) echo the industry's line.

A widely circulated newsletter not dependent upon advertising for its income began publishing life insurance articles a few years ago that could not have been better prepared by the Institute of Life Insurance. A family magazine boasting a circulation of more than 7 million published an article on life insurance in 1964 and another in 1967. Both articles, purporting to explain the mysteries of life insurance, preached the industry Cash Surrender Value gospel chapter and verse. Both publications did a brisk business in selling reprints of the articles to life insurance companies, which in turn supplied their salesmen with this "objective" information as an aid in convincing doubters.

The family magazine, incidentally, did some advertising of its own. Its "pro-permanent" article was displayed in a three-page spread in a widely circulated life insurance trade paper. The article was described as explaining the "facts" of life insurance "calmly, clearly, thoroughly . . . just the way one of your best agents would."

In order to conserve agent power, reprints could be had for a modest outlay—orders of more than 4,999: 3 cents each.

The Institute of Life Insurance does not concentrate its entire effort on "galvanizing" salesmen. It makes its appeal to the entire population, and some of the results were happily related by the *Life Association News* as follows:

> A Minneapolis teen-age student says to his father, "Dad, they taught us in social studies class this week that the head of the family should have at least five times his annual income in insurance. Do *we?*"
>
> A Wichita housewife inquires of her husband, "George, today's speaker at the family financial forum spent a long time talking about how you use permanent and term insurance. She said that the term should be used only when we could measure the length of the risk, because it might expire on us right when we needed it most. Don't you think we ought to convert our term and stick to ordinary life?"

A San Francisco editor orders his assistant, "Kill that dope story on life insurance profits. Doesn't the guy know that three quarters of the assets are in mutual companies and any savings go to the policyholder?"

How does it happen that teen-agers, businessmen, housewives, and editors are acquiring a bit of wisdom about this business? . . . It consists of a whole lifetime of articles read, headlines scanned, TV commercials dimly remembered, lectures heard, billboards noted, courses taken, and conversations exchanged.[4]

The Institute of Life Insurance kept its shoulder to the wheel in spreading these "bits of wisdom," *Life Association News* assured its readers. The Institute mailed out an average of 50,000 pieces of life insurance propaganda every working day of the year. It ran ads that "give people a warm feeling about the life insurance they own and a desire to ask their agents about what they might need to own."

In the same article, the *News* pointed out that 21 major consumer publications had carried 57 articles about life insurance the previous year, only one of which was unfavorable. Just what the Institute's part in this resounding journalistic vote of confidence was, the *News* did not say. It is interesting to note, however, that the one voice in the wilderness was described only as "unfavorable"—*not* inaccurate.

Chapter 25

Regulation

"If the general level of competence and dedication of all state commissioners sinks only a little lower, state regulation will be doomed." —Halsey D. Josephson, in *Probe*

The life insurance industry, the biggest financial institution in the United States, has never experienced Federal control and regulation. Efforts in this direction have cropped up over the years and, without exception, have been subdued. In 1868 a case involving life insurance reached the U.S. Supreme Court, and the resultant decision staved off the specter of Federal control for three-quarters of a century. In 1944 another case reached the high court, and life insurance was declared to be interstate commerce, which technically opened the door to the Federal Government. A massive lobbying effort resulted in keeping the federal government from entering into the regulation and control of the industry with the passing of the McCarran-Ferguson Act (Public Law 15) in 1945.

All governmental control and regulation of the industry is in the hands, individually, of the 50 states; which, in effect, leaves the industry largely self-regulated. In each state there is an insurance department and an insurance commissioner (or director), an arrangement that historically has run the gamut from abominable to something less than adequate. The insurance laws vary from state to state, and, as Edwin A. Patterson wrote in *The Insurance Commissioner in the United States,* "Insurance legislation tends to be standard-creating, rather than abuse-correcting."

Each state insurance commissioner must approve all new

policies offered by companies doing business in his state. If a policy contains provisions that a commissioner considers unfair, deceptive, misleading, unjust, or having a tendency to mislead or misrepresent, the policy may be disapproved. What one commissioner considers grounds for this decision may not sway another. Therefore, what may be considered unsuitable in one state could be sold in the other 49.

Just what constitutes deception, for example? No state insurance commissioner has ever considered it deceptive or misleading, or even tending to lead to misunderstanding, not to specifically spell out in a "permanent" policy that an increase in Cash Surrender Value means a proportionate *decrease* in the amount for which the company remains "on the risk."

It is within the power of a state insurance department to revoke an agent's license for misrepresentation, yet I can find no record of this ever having been done to any life insurance salesman who sells "permanent" life insurance through the misleading method of "net costing." The same applies to the free-wheeling guesswork involved in projecting the so-called "dividends" of participating policies.

The states do not have the power to set rates charged. The companies are free to set the commission rate paid to their salesmen (except in New York State, where the maximum allowed on the first year's premium is 55 percent), yet it could be considered strange that no regulatory office has ever questioned that the commission is paid not only on that part of the premium that buys pure death protection, but on the excess premium that goes into the Cash Surrender Value "savings account" as well.

The fact that state insurance departments do not attempt to correct these and other abuses does not, of course, mean that a Federal agency would do so. But the long, undistinguished history of state regulation certainly indicates the chances of reform are extremely rare if the system continues.

The corruption in state regulation played a part in bringing on the Armstrong Investigation in the early part of this century. The industry had become completely arrogant in its manipulation of state commissioners. Bribery was widespread where other methods proved inadequate. When public hearings could not be avoided, they were restrained. In 1885 one journalist took note of the "utter worthlessness of state supervision to protect the people against the impositions and deceit of dishonest officers and rotten insurance companies."

The actions of one New York commissioner, Louis Payn, led Governor "Teddy" Roosevelt—on the occasion of refusing to reappoint Payn on grounds of malfeasance—to remark sarcastically that "being a frugal man, out of the seven thousand dollars a year salary he has saved enough to borrow nearly half a million dollars from a trust company, the directors of which are also the directors of an insurance company."

Many commissioners were on insurance company payrolls, and it was almost axiomatic that a "good" commissioner would always be welcomed aboard as a company executive once his "public service" was done.

Life insurance men still move easily from the industry to the state insurance departments, and back. In addition, they are almost unanimous in their stand against Federal control, yet some are frustrated by the variations in insurance laws from one state to another. A general agent, writing in a trade journal, had this to say:

> I do not see how conscientious life insurance people can condone or tolerate these varying State Government infringements on our right to sell whatever our good companies offer for sale any other place in these United States.[1]

Statements such as this, intentional or not, are out-and-out invitations to Federal control, for if the insurance laws of one state could be superseded by those of another state, this

would necessitate a Federal insurance code and an agency
to oversee it.

An outspoken critic of continuation of state regulation
has been *Probe* editor Halsey D. Josephson, who wrote:

> The main problem is not the absence of the desire [to
> act], but rather a high degree of helplessness in the face of
> enormous economic and legal complexities. . . . The ques-
> tion of federal vs. state regulation is no longer one of prefer-
> ence. It has become a matter of inevitability.[2]

Earlier, Josephson stated:

> The public, being both uninformed and apathetic, will
> not initiate correction. When all is said and done, only the
> state departments can save life insurance from the insatiable
> companies themselves, and they simply aren't going to do it.
> As far as we are concerned, enlightened, public-spirited,
> federal regulation can't come soon enough. How long are we
> going to kid ourselves about the virtues of state supervision
> when we know in our hearts that, in the main, it is unpro-
> ductive, unwieldy, uninspired, understaffed, underpaid, and
> frequently, uninformed?
>
> Is it possible that some prefer it because of its limi-
> tations?[3]

The limitations may not only be preferable; they may also
be intentional. Insurance laws coming before state legislatures emanate from insurance committees, and these committees are invariably made up almost in their entirety of men
in the insurance business, whose vested interest is directly
opposed to any constriction of that industry.

The National Association of Insurance Commissioners

If the whole is the sum of its individual parts, the National
Association of Insurance Commissioners (NAIC) paints a

rather pathetic picture of the condition of insurance regulation and control. This organization, as the name implies, is composed of the insurance commissioners of each of the 50 states. An unofficial group, it holds meetings twice each year on a national basis, ostensibly to hash over the heavy burdens of public responsibility the commissioners shoulder individually. It is, in fact, the closest thing to a central bulwark against the self-interest of the life insurance industry that the American public has. In this role, it leaves a great deal to be desired.

For example, on November 30, 1964, 50 insurance commissioners converged on the quiet little Western hamlet of Las Vegas, Nevada, in order to share their thoughts in proper seclusion on how best to serve the public interest. Some few kill-joys attempted to cast a pall over the proceedings. The *Insurance Field,* for example, editorialized dourly:

> The glow of "Glitter Gulch" cast the winter meeting of the NAIC in a glare which, according to reports, made everyone just a bit uncomfortable but left them still able to work a little in this city dedicated to pleasure.

High on the agenda was a piece of business left over from the previous summer's convention in Minneapolis, to wit: whether to hold a future meeting in Hawaii. The decision was eventually tabled. Another item which demanded and got action was the completion of a model regulatory proposal having to do with the solicitation of insurance stock proxies and model legislation covering insider trading of life insurance stocks. This, significantly, was something that *had* to be done in order to maintain the exemption of insurance from Securities and Exchange Commission regulation.

A matter of interest to life insurance buyers appeared briefly on the agenda. Someone suggested that the unavailability of renewable term life insurance be looked into, but the same individual apparently had misgivings and asked that the item be deleted from the agenda. Consequently, renewable term continued to be "unavailable."

Other issues before the 50 commissioners and their cast of over 1,950 were not so urgent, and were for the most part tabled for further discussion at a future date. Here is how the *National Underwriter* covered the event:

> These meetings are the forum for give and take between the industry and its regulators. There is a distinct tendency on the part of the industry to maintain a hard brake on any sort of change which appears to be imminent or even slightly drastic.

This "give and take" went on for five days, with the merrymakers giving and Las Vegas taking. The promise of the previous convention in Minneapolis died on the vine. At that conclave there had also been fun and games galore for the only 1,400 in attendance, with nothing accomplished in the way of the public's (your) interest and very little in the interest of the industry, except to keep the "brakes" on. The *National Underwriter,* ever hopeful, had mused at the time:

> Yet in its activities in Minneapolis NAIC laid the groundwork for considerable business at its next meeting . . . at Las Vegas. And the fact that so much seems to be due for the winter agenda may help take away the curse some people said they feel attached to a meeting for business purposes in a city that emphasizes something less than dull toil.

Behind the Mask

The real fear the life insurance industry has of Federal regulation is not to be found in the standard phrases of "creeping socialism," "states' rights," or "government being better close to home." It is a deep-seated fear that strong, central regulation of life insurance—similar to that which the Securities and Exchange Commission exercises over the investment field—will lead to full disclosure of what makes it so profitable—in particular, the disclosure of its true price. Selling methods would have to be changed if this were the case, and some life insurance men would rather switch than face this prospect. Harry V. Wade, president of Standard Life of Indiana, a 40-year veteran of the life insurance business, was quoted in the *National Underwriter* as saying: ". . . if we have to live under SEC regulation of our selling methods, I'll sell off our in-force and go into the banana business." [4]

Full disclosure of the cost of life insurance could only be accomplished by showing the cost of pure death protection separated from all the trimmings involved in "permanent" Cash Surrender Value insurance. There is small wonder that the industry quakes at the thought of any such revelation.

Dr. Joseph M. Belth, in his authoritative *The Retail Price Structure in American Life Insurance,* pointed out that widespread price disclosure could "conceivably undermine the concept of level-premium life insurance." Rather than see this catastrophe take place, Dr. Belth suggested a system for

> gradual disclosure of a company's price structure over a period of twenty years, at the end of which time total disclosure would have been accomplished. . . . The gradual disclosure of prices would permit a company, if necessary, to adjust its operations in order to present an attractive price structure. In this manner, the potential disruptive effect of price disclosure perhaps could be largely avoided.[5]

Twenty years, it would seem, is a long time to ask the American public to wait for the life insurance industry to fully disclose the facts about its price structure.

Forbes magazine, in its December 1, 1966, issue, ran an article entitled: "The Insurance Industry: Next in Line?" It sounded a portentous note for the industry:

Like the auto industry, the tire industry, packaging and mutual funds before it, the long nearly sacrosanct insurance business is likely soon to feel the protect-the-consumer reformist zeal of the U.S. Congress.

Among other things, the ability of the states to regulate the sprawling giant was questioned:

To what extent is it regulated *effectively* by the states? Some states, with New York the admitted leader, take the regulatory responsibility very seriously indeed. But others, like Texas and Pennsylvania, are so lax as to have become a happy hunting ground for promoters and fast-buck artists. . . . In any case, inherent in the system is an unevenness of regulation, in that a company may be forbidden to do in one state what it is permitted in the next; and certain kinds of companies—the mail order outfits, for example—are often, in effect, run without any regulation at all.

The question of full disclosure was also brought up in the *Forbes* article:

. . . suppose the life insurance companies were required by federal law or regulation to make really full disclosure to policyholders—as publicly owned corporations must? Would the conventional life insurance salesman be able to cope with this complication? [6]

Some men in government are, hopefully, more interested in the right of the public to know what it is buying than worrying about a salesman's ability to cope with having to reveal the true facts. Such men have failed to appear on the scene at the state regulatory level, which leaves only one alternative. If the regulation of the life insurance industry passes from state to Federal hands, and if this is considered to be a loss of states' rights, then it can only be called a loss by default.

Chapter 26

The Salesman

"Finally, we try to instill in our men the unalterable, unshakable
belief that the guy on the other side of the desk has $200 of our
man's money in his pocket. Now, if he has $200 of my dough in
his pocket, I don't believe I'd say, 'Aw, come on, gimme my
$200.' Hell, no! I'd attack him with all the strength at my dis-
posal, with the tenacity of a bull dog, a real tiger. My chances
of getting the $200 increase with my persuasive powers."

—John R. Humphries,
Massachusetts Mutual general agent, Atlanta, Georgia,
in *The National Underwriter*, Feb. 27, 1965

Standing between you and the home offices of America's
life insurance companies is something known generally as
the American agency system. This consists of regional and
local agencies for the companies, each under the supervision
of a general agent or manager. It is out of these organizations
that the salesman operates.

The recruiting program that the American agency system
is continuously engaged in would put to shame the com-
bined efforts of Army, Navy, Marines, and the used-car business. The reason for this is the incredibly high casualty rate
among men who go into life insurance sales, an occupation
which has been called the "most agonizing person-to-person
sales duel in the United States."

One company alone over a nine-year period recruited
5,000 new salesmen, yet at the end of the nine years the
net increase in the sales force was only 50; 4,950 had not
been able to stand the gaff. The industry does not realistically
expect the condition to improve. Only one thing is expected
from the new man, and that is the "natural market" he brings

with him—relatives, friends, acquaintances, lodge brothers, and so on.

Where do life insurance rookies come from? Among college students life insurance ranks near the bottom of career preferences. Dean Ernest C. Arbuckle of Stanford University's Graduate School of Business said that his impression was "students feel insurance is 'hard sell' in the image of the life insurance agent telephoning and soliciting business, believe it pays poorly to start, is not competitive with other industries, offers slow progress and no intellectual challenge." [1]

Few men go from college into life insurance sales. Most recruits have tried their hand at other jobs, and many wind up in the business out of desperation. It is, as one insurance executive said, either life insurance or else.

As for the industry, its efforts at recruiting have at times approached the ridiculous. Probably the most bizarre example in the entire history of recruiting was an effort charged to a major company by a magazine in 1900. The Belgian manager of the company reportedly planned to engage the Pope as a general agent. The Pontiff was to be on a first-year commission of 38 percent, and his territory was to be the entire earth.[2]

Learning the Business

Training is usually minimal before the new man is turned loose on the public. A general agent for one of the country's largest companies declared that he expected any full-time agent to be "in the field his first day." "In the field" means that he is ready to plan your estate for you. Other general agents seriously question such extreme haste and advise a period of training for all new salesmen.

LIAMA—Life Insurance Agency Management Association—made a study which revealed that in many large urban agencies the recruit received less than three hours per week in training and supervision during his first six months, the most critical months in the business.

With the high turnover in men, the agencies figure they cannot afford expensive training for a man who is not likely to last anyway. So he is given a hasty course of instruction in the virtues of "permanent" Cash Surrender Value life insurance, and is told to compile a list of everyone he knows on a first-name basis. The recruit starts off with his family, friends, and so on down the line until he has at least a hundred names. The agency then has his name printed on their standard announcement form, and this is mailed to everyone on the list proclaiming the launching of the new career.

The announcement that Cousin Willie or good old Joe is now with Friendly Life usually is received with something less than enthusiasm. The new man himself discovers this soon enough. He is put off with excuses, friends jaywalk to avoid him, and he soon begins to fall into a mild depression of spirit. The general agent pumps him back up, helps him with his phone calls from the agency "bullpen," even goes along with him when an appointment can be made.

The weeks and months drag by. The list begins to dwindle. But sales *are* made. A $1,000 20-pay may be unloaded on a sympathetic friend, or a $5,000 endowment at 55 on a well-to-do uncle (please, *no* term insurance!), and by the time the "natural market" list has petered out, the first real challenge arises. This is where the sheep are separated from the goats. The great majority discover at this point that life insurance as a career is not for them. By the time a year has passed, 70 percent of the new men are gone. Fifteen percent of the remainder hang on by their fingernails for a year or two more.

What was it the agency was looking for in the new men? A survey by one trade journal showed that of 21 large companies contacted, 19 of them were most interested in this "natural market" that the new man could bring them. An article on recruiting in the *National Underwriter* mentioned other hoped-for qualities.

> Does he have sales talent? Sales talent is, of course, the most important. Does he have the guts to stay with the business during the difficult early days? Is he persistent, tenacious, and does he have that shark or killer instinct we look for in the strong salesman? [3]

Hucksters or Professionals?

After three years we find a residue of persistent, tenacious men. They have now arrived at the point where they would like to have status or recognized professional standing. In other words, trying to divest the life insurance salesman of the huckster image and make him respectable is the goal. President Orville E. Beal, of the Prudential, told a meeting of the Life Insurance Advertisers Association:

> If we can bring the public to understand that the well-trained insurance agent *is* a professional, then we will create more respect and consequently more receptivity for him when he sits down with his prospects. We will have done something to make this sales duel a little less agonizing.
> However, we cannot do this effectively until we have defined exactly what we mean by the agent's professionalism. We must have no doubt about this concept, for doubt would lead to hesitation and vacillation in its use. . . . So, then, what do we mean when we say the agent is a professional? It means an expert, one who knows what he is doing and does it well. [4]

Life insurance men hit upon the idea of tacking some letters onto their names, *à la* M.D., D.D.S., LL.B., etc. They came up with C.L.U., which stands for Chartered Life Underwriter. Sophistication was added when they also dropped the title "life insurance salesman."

Some insurance men, however, scoff at this gilding of the lily. Roger Martel, Montreal agency manager of Alliance Mutual Life Insurance Company, had this to say:

> In my many years of experience, I have never noticed so much camouflage, so many disguises. More and more successful agents now call themselves estate consultants, investment counsellors, savings analysts, pension specialists. There are less and less life insurance company representatives! [5]

Consider a couple of the ten fundamental factors of a successful company (and successful agents) that President Harry S. McConachie, of American Mutual Life of Iowa, set before a LIAMA conference in Chicago:

1. Push hard for quality business. It's the payoff for agents, and agents need more money. . . .
2. Push for cash value sales. They are worth paying bonuses for.[6]

There appears to be small, if any, concern for the public in the foregoing statements. Commenting editorially on the matter of professionalism, the *National Underwriter* said:

> But in a business where agents must sell to eat, it is hardly feasible to bring them to a truly professional level of knowledge and skill before turning them loose on the public. However, a professional attitude is something else. Even the rank novice can have it—and should. For it is not the lack of knowledge and skill that will cause the public to detect an embarrassing gap between claims and performance. Rather it is a lack of professional attitude.[7]

But what of the hapless public upon which this rank novice with the all-important "professional attitude" has been turned loose? The gap between claims and performance will prove to be far more than embarrassing when widows and children discover that their late husbands' and fathers' life insurance was completely fouled up by this agent who "had to eat" regardless of what havoc he wrought in writing policies for his clients. It will be a tragedy.

In the same editorial, *National Underwriter* pointed out a lurking danger to the agent as his image of professionalism grew when it noted an

> increasing tendency to hold the agent responsible in damages for giving incorrect advice or failing to do what he said he would. . . . As the professional image of the agent continues to be imprinted on the public mind, it will be increasingly difficult to duck the responsibilities that go with professional status.

Where the Money Is

A man selling anything, be it life insurance or automobiles, can scarcely be considered an impartial adviser so long as his remuneration depends upon commission. He will, quite naturally, drive for the biggest sale possible, and will push that sample of his product which carries the highest commission rate.

The man who pushes "permanent" Cash Surrender Value life insurance cannot sell the low-price product and long prosper. Unfortunately for the public, that low-price product, which is pure death protection, or term insurance, is what the public needs.

One of the fastest-growing companies in the country is Franklin Life, a firm specializing in individual "permanent"

insurance. The agents of Franklin Life seem to have an un-
controllable urge to write paeans of gratitude to the vice
president of their company, Mr. F. J. O'Brien (affectionately
called "O.B."), while he, in turn, appears to be so moved
by these letters that he cannot resist the urge to have them
published in the form of advertisements in trade journals—
intended, incidentally, to woo disgruntled salesmen away from
less happy companies. Here are a few excerpts from such
letters:

> *"More Money than I Ever Dared Dream!"* effused Mr. H.
> Wayne Hamm of Bloomington, Illinois, on March 28, 1967.
> From a beginning income in 1961 of $3,616.41, he had
> [risen]—through selling "permanent" insurance—to $33,-
> 652.72 only 5 years later, and still climbing.

> *"Income beyond my fondest dreams!"* glowed Mr. Ralph H.
> Jinkens, [whose income] had reached the $18,170.08 plateau.

> *"Muchas gracias . . . wonderful things have happened to*
> *me"* purred bi-lingual Doel R. Garcia from sunny Ponce,
> Puerto Rico, citing a $6,512.87 income for 1963 which
> through the miracle of Franklin Life shot up to a respectable
> $80,110.79 in 1965.

The people at Franklin have reason to be proud of all this
prosperity they have created through the sale of "permanent"
life insurance. A nit-picker, however, might scratch his head
and wonder where all the letters of praise from the *policyholders* are.

As a matter of fact, Franklin Life can afford to be friendly.
In another trade-journal appeal for more high-volume producers to desert their present companies and come "where
the profit is," agency Vice President William D. Clements re-

vealed some interesting statistics on the earnings of their top 500 agents. It read as follows:

	Average for 1965
1st 10	$136,853.58
1st 25	$ 95,887.76
1st 50	$ 69,014.15
1st 100	$ 50,350.03
1st 200	$ 36,275.41
1st 500	$ 22,621.06

The first ten producers for Franklin Life made more money in 1965 than the salary paid the President of the United States, and these amounts are authenticated "as reported to the Internal Revenue Service." Every dime of it came directly from the premiums paid by their policyholders, extracted from that part of the premium buying death protection and that part supposedly being deposited in the "savings account."

Knights of the Million Dollar Round Table

"After developing their yodeling skills, over 2,000 Million Dollar Round Table members and their families were prepared for fine cheese, alpenstocks and high-level insurance talk this month in Switzerland."

Thus reported the *Life Association News* on the occasion of the Million Dollar Round Table's fortieth-anniversary get-together in faraway Lucerne in the summer of 1967.

The Million Dollar Round Table is the elite corps of the life insurance selling fraternity. The requirement, as indicated, is the sale of a million dollars or more in life insurance coverage in a single year. There is one catch, however, that might keep you from getting the proper death protection from one of these men, and that is the fact that the less costly forms of life insurance do not count at full face value toward membership in the Round Table. The would-be Knight who sells what this book recommends—Decreasing Term to Age 65—will have to sell as much as $6,666,666.67 of it to meet the sales-volume requirements of the club.

The Round Table is an organization within the National Association of Life Underwriters, and the Association's code of ethics has as its second item of an agent's responsibility: *"To keep my clients' needs always uppermost."*

Where It All Comes From

Pure death protection, or term insurance, is the outcast of the life insurance industry. The man who pushes it in favor of the far more lucrative "permanent" plans is looked down upon by his fellows as something less than smart. The real money comes from their "permanent" insurance, which, as we have already seen, is simply nothing more than *their* way of selling buy-term-and-invest-the-difference. It is the "difference" that throws off the huge commissions, the mink coats and other gifts that accrue to top flight salesmen.

The giving of plush prizes and awards has risen to such extremes that some people within the industry have reacted unfavorably. *Probe,* under the heading "Nothing Like Mink," commented sharply regarding a particular case:

> Very likely it all began with flowers for the wife of the leading producer of the month. But we've come a long way since that innocuous beginning. A press release just received informs us that 23 wives received mink stoles from a life insurance company as rewards for their husbands' success in a company campaign; and, perhaps to provide them with an opportunity to display their new finery, they were awarded

also, together with their husbands, all-expense-paid vacations to a famous resort.

We don't know whether our stomachs turned at the nature of the prizes or at the absurdity of broadcasting the news. In either event, we earnestly recommend that all companies and agencies indulging in such distasteful performances make them top-drawer secrets—unless, of course, their object is to get the public to detest them.[8]

Tricks of the Trade

The music starts and the small screen comes alive in full color. Ten minutes later the music fades, the show is over, and another prospect has been exposed to *Man's Golden Hands.* The Production National Life salesman hovers close by readying the application for his "Golden Accumulator" policy. An article in *Best's Life News* revealed that Production National's batting average jumped from one in four closings to three in four, due to the show-and-tell box. "If an agent has shown the film to his prospect and the call lasts longer than 30 minutes," agent Arnold Ursprung was quoted as saying, "then you are either just visiting or the prospect is not ready to buy." [9]

The success of the movie in the company's home state of Texas was such that President Wade B. Campbell envisioned the spread of Production National's cinematic gospel. "Armed with 8-mm films, our agents will go beyond Texas in 1966, to other states," Campbell reportedly said.

Audio-visual selling devices such as this are becoming more and more widespread in life insurance, but there are many who prefer to rely on tried and true techniques. Mr. Hal L. Nutt, CLU, Director of the Life Insurance Marketing Institute at Purdue University, in a regular column in the *Insurance Field,* advises the use of fear as a selling tool. Wrote Nutt:

Death is a morbid subject, and you don't like it. Neither, you feel, does the prospect like it, and you refuse to back the hearse up to the prospect's door. Well, I agree. I don't think we should back the hearse up to the prospect's door— I think we should put him *in* it! The prospect buys life insurance when he becomes afraid of the consequences of death. We've got to "kill" him.[10]

Nutt, in another column, after "killing" the prospect and putting him in the hearse, has now taken him to Forest Lawn and buried him. He recommends this pitch to the men in the field:

Mr. Prospect, after you're dead and the funeral is over, all your good friends and relatives will come to your house to pay respects to your wife and family. They will bring food and flowers and cry real tears and sincerely and absolutely feel bad that you have passed, leaving your wife a widow and your children fatherless. However, with all these lovely thoughts, and with all these material things they will bring, no one will bring money but me, Mr. Prospect—and I don't even know your wife. But you can always depend upon the insurance man to bring money if you at least plan for it ahead of time. This is the time that you should plan for it.[11]

This *is* the time to plan for it, but you should tell Mr. Salesman that the only kind of money you want him to bring your widow is pure death protection dollars.

There are endless nuances to the business of selling life insurance. Les O'Neil, a salesman with Kansas City Life, made a suggestion regarding the possible wariness of a prospect when a field supervisor or manager comes along with the agent on a call. In the *Insurance Salesman*, O'Neil told of his brain child:

Here's how it is done! The agent approaches the house, leaving the supervisor in the car. (The supervisor should keep a light on in the car.) He can try to let the prospect see the other fellow in the car, but if that fails, he remarks to the prospect, "I can only stay about 15 minutes. I have another agent in the car and we have another appointment." I cannot think of anyone who will not, out of common courtesy, invite the other fellow in rather than let him sit in the car. The supervisor should sit quietly for at least a little while into the interview, then break in with: "I have only one problem, and that is being able to sit quietly during an interview. I think I might be able to clear this (or that) up with John Agent's permission." Now you're in and the prospect himself actually invited you in. Before too long, you should call the office number and say, "Mrs. Prospect, I'm sorry, but I'll be a little late" (feigning a call to your next appointment). Then say, "Oh, your husband can't be there anyway? Well, suppose we make it about 7:30 tomorrow or Thursday? Tomorrow's okay? Good, see you then!" Don't miss this part or your prospect may smell something fishy.[12]

They are clever, and they have had more than a century to work out their techniques of going through, over, under, and around your defenses. It is undeniable that most men need death protection, and all these—and thousands more—selling devices would be entirely justified if life insurance salesmen would sell only *pure* life insurance.

Chapter 27

Home Offices—The Edifice Complex

"A sentiment quite independent of the need for space impelled the company chieftains to vie with each other in erecting impressive edifices."—Morton Keller, *The Life Insurance Enterprise*

In the late nineteenth century the giants of life insurance—Henry Hyde of Equitable, John Dryden of Prudential, Joseph Knapp of Metropolitan, and others—took a look around and what they saw made them feel left out. Immensely rich though their companies were, they had no belching smokestacks, no gleaming steel rails stretching across the country, no blast furnaces; in short, no real outward manifestation of their wealth and power.

Out of this frustration the Home Office syndrome was born. Obviously, any business has to have a place in which to carry on its work. But the life insurance business is unlike any other. It works under a socio-religious cloak, purportedly sparing no effort to provide the life insurance needed by Americans at the very minimum cost possible.

In an industry known for its excesses, others were now in the offing. The Prudential rationalized it all with a note of pure selflessness and good intent when, in the words of President Dryden, it was explained that the new home office was to "typify and symbolize the character of the business of Prudential, [and] exemplify its all pervading spirit of beneficence and its ingrained love of the golden rule."

In 1890 construction began in Newark, New Jersey. The design was based on a French château which had stood on the

181

River Loire, a high-turreted, gray-stone building. It was to be the biggest building in New Jersey by the time it was completed in 1892. A great celebration was held on the occasion, with Prudential men coming from hundreds of miles around, and the nearly 4,000 people of the home office staff staging a parade through the streets of Newark, with no less than five military bands. President Dryden himself reviewed the troops from a stand, while another company officer, Peter Egenoff, wearing a white sash, led them on a white charger.

The Prudential building resembled a cathedral, while the New York Life home office had an entrance "resembling an ancient temple—and a temple it is—A Temple of Humanity." [1]

The Metropolitan home office, in New York's Madison Square, was to be the grandest of them all. The furnishings alone for President John Hegeman's office cost $90,000 (and the dollar of that day was worth five of today's). A history of the company said of the new home office:

> It was an imposing building, of white marble, rich and delicately carved and gracefully decorated. The main entrance led to the magnificent court and marble stairway, where the designers had lavished their finest materials. Its height and bulk of marble alone would have made it impressive; and to this the architects added a double staircase and a bronze and onyx balustrade rising in sweeping curves to a colonnaded open loggia above. The Board of Directors' Room on the second floor was no less imposing—here, said a contemporary journal, was a "Rembrandt feeling, typical of conservativeness, which would invite calm deliberation on the part of its occupants." [2]

Metropolitan topped the whole thing off with its famous tower, then the tallest on earth.

The building spree spread out from home offices into regional offices. As investments, the buildings were poor. But this made little difference, for in the long run they were expected to pay for themselves indirectly.

Expense—then or now—in the building of home offices for life insurance companies has served an additional purpose. An article in a trade journal explained it this way:

> Insurers are proud of their home offices, and rightly so. We tend to picture them in sales promotion material, or on letterheads, or in other ways. Along comes Emerson Q. Insured and he makes a snap judgment by means of that picture. He equates insurance with money, and money with home office size. A big home office means a large amount of money.[3]

Oh, yes, Emerson Q. Insured, it *does* mean a large amount of money. And if you happen to be one of the policyholders, you have put—and are putting—in more than is required under any stretch of the imagination.

Times have not changed. Only the building materials. Suppose our friend Emerson Q. Insured was a policyholder of Phoenix Mutual Life Insurance Company. Perhaps back in 1940 he saw one of Phoenix' ads telling how to retire with $150 a month, and he bought the policy. Emerson by now has discovered that the $150 a month doesn't quite do the job (so has Phoenix, as the most recent ad has lifted the figure to $300 a month), but he can look with pride on the new home office on American Row in the heart of Hartford, Connecticut. The building is a lenticular hyperboloid, which seems to mean it is shaped like a very tall ship. Graceful, sided with cool green glass, it stands poised in a pool of water as if preparing to sail away. The pool itself is lined with 44,000 pounds of lead so that it will not drain into the crews' cars in the garage below.

All this aesthetic modern architecture may be beautiful,

but it does not help Emerson Q. Insured retire on $150 a month.

There are hundreds of others, from the Connecticut General Life Building in downtown Los Angeles (the tallest in Southern California) to the 100-story John Hancock Building in Chicago (the tallest building in the world outside New York City) to the amazing Prudential Center and 52-story Prudential Building in Boston (the tallest building outside New York City, *before* John Hancock).

Many are self-contained communities, with all the necessities required by man, as well as most of the non-necessities. Employees are kept happy and, in some cases, well fed. Metropolitan, since 1869, has provided free lunch for all employees and officers in its home office. Like every other expense in running an insurance company, all this and more is reflected in the premiums paid by the policyholders.

Home Offices, as one writer put it, are a monument to the gullibility of the common man.

Chapter 28

Epilogue

". . . the implications of a sudden requirement for virtually total price disclosures are staggering. . . . Widespread price disclosure could conceivably undermine the concept of level-premium life insurance."

—Dr. Joseph M. Belth, CLU, CPCU,
The Retail Price Structure in American Life Insurance

Elizur Wright, recognized as the father of American life insurance, once looked on his child and sadly remarked that he was "persuaded that life insurance was the most available, convenient, and permanent breeding place for rogues that civilization had ever presented." [1] A century later a clergyman, Dr. John Sutherland Bonnell, voiced an entirely different view of the industry when he said: "It is doubtful if any other form of business enterprise in our entire economy is more surely grounded on moral and spiritual principles or offers larger scope for their practice than does the noble institution of life insurance." [2]

Somewhere between these two extremes lies the truth.

The "noble institution" of life insurance is firmly grounded on the perpetuation of a monumental myth. Its fundamental concept—level-premium, "permanent," Cash Surrender Value life insurance—by its very nature demands that the true cost of death protection under such plans be kept from the buying public in order that the concept itself may continue to exist. The unbelievable complexities that have arisen have not only hidden this vital information, but in the process have completely buried the real purpose of life insurance.

Full disclosure of the cost of life insurance can only come about by separating the death protection from the so-called "savings" or "investment" represented by Cash Surrender Values. When—and if—this disclosure comes, this system of "permanent" life insurance will die a natural death.

The men who control the industry have always been keenly aware of this and have worked with great success to ward off all efforts at true regulation and control of their industry, which would have to begin with this full disclosure. It is obvious that the life insurance industry will not—in fact, *cannot*— change voluntarily. The chance that change will come about involuntarily through governmental action is equally remote because of the tremendous economic and political powers the industry wields. Until such time as the American public becomes fully aware of the real facts about life insurance, with all its misleading concepts, and gimmicks, and makes this awareness vociferously known to its elected representatives, the status quo is all that can honestly be expected.

While waiting for this to happen, however, the individual can exercise effective "self-control" of his own. Full understanding of what life insurance is, what it can and cannot do— all hopefully provided by this book—will enable the individual to by-pass the booby traps of "permanent" Cash Surrender Value life insurance, and seek out the pure, reasonably priced, death protection he needs and can afford.

Notes

Chapter 1. Cash Surrender Value—Root of the Evil

1. *The Economics of Life Insurance*, by Solomon S. Huebner; 3rd edition, New York: Appleton-Century-Crofts, Inc., 1959, p. 191.
2. *Life Insurance*, by Joseph B. Maclean; 7th edition, 2nd impression; New York: McGraw-Hill Book Co., Inc., 1951, p. 14.
3. *Modern Life Insurance—A Textbook of Income Insurance*, by Robert I. Mehr and Robert W. Osler; revised edition: 3rd printing, New York: The Macmillan Co., 1959, p. 117 footnotes.
4. *Life Insurance Fact Book; 1966*, published annually by the Institute of Life Insurance, pp. 17, 25, 29, 57.
5. Maclean, *op. cit.,* p. 114.
6. *Marketing Life Insurance—Its History in America*, by Dr. J. Owen Stalson; Cambridge: Harvard University Press, 1942, p. 644.
7. *Life and Life Insurance*, by Griffin M. Lovelace; published by Life Insurance Agency Management Association, Hartford, Conn., 1961, p. 213.
8. *Ibid.,* p. 269.
9. *The Retail Price Structure in American Life Insurance*, by Dr. Joseph M. Belth; Bloomington: Indiana University Press, 1966, p. 243.

Chapter 2. Cash Surrender Value and Foregone Interest

1. *National Underwriter* (NALU Convention Daily), September 15, 1965, p. 24.
2. Joseph B. Maclean, in *Eastern Underwriter*, October 7, 1927.
3. *National Underwriter*, June 22, 1963, pp. 1, 8, 9.
4. *The Retail Price Structure in American Life Insurance*, by Dr. Joseph M. Belth; Bloomington: Indiana University Press, 1966, p. 37.

Chapter 3. Cash Surrender Value—The Phantom Tax Dodge

1. Alfred N. Guertin, from *National Underwriter*, October 17, 1964.
2. *Life Insurance Fundamentals*, by Griffin M. Lovelace, revised

   edition; New York: Harper & Brothers, Publishers, 1923, 1925,
   p. 223.
3. *Life Insurance,* by S. S. Huebner; 5th edition, p. 524.
4. From a survey made by Sounding Board, an independent research organization.
5. *National Underwriter,* December 4, 1964, p. 4.
6. American Institute of Economic Research, "What Would More
   Inflation Mean to You?" *Economic Education Bulletin,* Vol. VI,
   No. 4, July, 1966, pp. 72–73.
7. *Ibid.*
8. *World Insurance Trends,* edited by Davis W. Gregg and Dan M.
   McGill; proceedings of the First International Insurance Conference, Philadelphia, Pa., May, 1957; University of Pennsylvania
   Press, p. 134.
9. *Ibid.,* pp. 125–126.

Chapter 4. Cash Surrender Value—History

1. *Insurance Field Magazine,* January 18, 1963.
2. *The Great Stewardship—A Story of Life Insurance, by* Albert W.
   Atwood; New York: Harper & Brothers, Publishers, 1945, p. 166.
3. *Marketing Life Insurance—Its History in America,* by Dr. J.
   Owen Stalson; Cambridge, Harvard University Press, 1942.
4. *Ibid.,* pp. 420–421.
5. *Ibid.,* pp. 487–488.
6. *The Life Insurance Enterprise, 1885–1910,* by Morton Keller;
   Cambridge: the Belknap Press of Harvard University Press, 1963,
   p. 57.
7. *Ibid.,* p. 202.
8. Stalson, *op. cit.,* p. 423.
9. Keller, *op. cit.,* p. 240.
10. *Ibid.,* p. 240.
11. *Ibid.,* p. 253.

Chapter 5. The Cost Is Prohibitive

1. *Modern Life Insurance—A Textbook of Income Insurance,* by
   Robert I. Mehr and Robert W. Osler; revised edition, 3rd printing,
   New York: the Macmillan Co., 1959, p. 28.
2. *National Underwriter,* editorial comment, September 24, 1966,
   p. 32.
3. *Life and Life Insurance,* by Griffin M. Lovelace, published by
   Life Insurance Agency Management Association, Hartford, Conn.,
   1961, p. 108.
4. Mehr and Osler, *op. cit.,* p. 558.

Chapter 6. Getting the Cash from Cash Surrender Value

1. Sheppard Homans, quoted in *Your Pocketbook Is Leaking*, by K. P. Chartier, 1958.
2. Ned Loar, CLU, *Life Association News*, June, 1967, p. 89, in a review of a Consumers Union series critical of permanent life insurance. Loar stated in his review of the three-part series that he had read only one installment.
3. Dudley Dowell, quoted in *Best's Life News*, January, 1967, pp. 41–42.

Chapter 7. Other Nonforfeitures—Paid-up and Extended Term

1. *Life Insurance,* by Joseph B. Maclean; 7th edition, 2nd impression; New York: McGraw-Hill Book Co., Inc., 1951, p. 202.

Chapter 8. Life Insurance—Sideline of the Industry

1. Robert B. Pitcher, in *National Underwriter*, March 7, 1964, p. 2.

Chapter 9. What to Buy

1. Oliver de Werthern, quoted in *Your Pocketbook Is Leaking*, by K. P. Chartier, 1958, p. 80.

Chapter 11. What to Do about Cash Surrender Value

1. *Life Insurance Fact Book*, published by the Institute of Life Insurance, 1966 edition, p. 57.
2. *National Underwriter*, December 9, 1961.
3. *Life Insurance: A Legalized Racket*, by Mort Gilbert and E. Albert Gilbert; Philadelphia: Marlowe Publishing Co., 1936, p. 16.
4. *National Underwriter*, November 4, 1961, p. 5.

Chapter 12. The "Conversion" Game

1. *Modern Life Insurance—A Textbook of Income Insurance*, by Robert I. Mehr and Robert W. Osler; revised edition, New York: the Macmillan Co., 1959, p. 696.
2. *National Underwriter*, July 9, 1966, p. 10.
3. *Forbes* magazine, May 1, 1965, p. 24.
4. *American Agency Bulletin*, May, 1963, p. 47.
5. Letter to Agent Thomas P. Fuller from Republic National Life Insurance Company, Dallas, Texas, dated July 7, 1965.

6. *National Underwriter,* May 28, 1966.
7. As quoted in *What's Wrong with Your Life Insurance,* by Norman F. Dacey; New York: Crowell-Collier Press, 1963, p. 349.

Chapter 13. How to Buy Your Pure Death Protection

1. *Insurance Field Magazine,* October 9, 1964, p. 28.

Chapter 14. Group Insurance

1. *National Underwriter,* October 23, 1965, p. 8.
2. *Forbes* magazine, July 15, 1967, p. 53.

Chapter 15. Insurance for Women

1. Miss Amy Vanderbilt's column, "Modern Manners," in the Atlanta *Constitution,* July 21, 1967.
2. *How Life Insurance Can Serve You,* by M. Albert Linton; New York: Harper & Brothers, Publishers, 1958, p. 26.
3. *The Insurance Salesman,* March, 1967, p. 118.

Chapter 16. Kiddie Kontracts and Family Policies

1. *223 Effective Approaches,* by Raymond C. McClintock; Indianapolis, Indiana: the Rough Notes Company, 1960, pp. 19, 20.
2. *National Underwriter,* June 5, 1965, p. 22.
3. *Newsweek* Magazine, September 6, 1965, p. 8.
4. *Forbes* magazine, June 1, 1966, p. 5.
5. *Probe,* February 13, 1961, pp. 3, 4.
6. *Newsweek* Magazine, September 14, 1964.

Chapter 17. Mutual Companies

1. *Life Insurance Stocks: The Modern Gold Rush,* by Arthur Milton; New York: Citadel Press, 1963, p. 34.
2. *Business Week* magazine, February 26, 1966, p. 80.
3. *Report of the Joint Committee of the Senate and Assembly of the State of New York* (Armstrong Committee), February 22, 1906, Albany, New York.
4. *A Study of Mutual Life Insurance Dividends,* by Frank S. J. McIntosh; National Analytical Services, Inc., 1961.
5. *Vice President in Charge of Revolution,* by Murray D. Lincoln as told to David Karp; New York: McGraw-Hill Book Co., Inc., 1960, p. 229.
6. *Finance,* August, 1966, p. 60.
7. McIntosh, *op. cit.,* p. 67.

Chapter 18. The "Net Cost" Farce

1. *Better Homes and Gardens,* July, 1964.
2. *Probe,* November 10, 1958.
3. *Life Insurance: Trends and Problems,* edited by David McCahan, Ph.D. (CLU); Philadelphia: University of Pennsylvania Press, 1943, p. 133.
4. *Discrimination: A Study of Recent Developments in American Life Insurance,* by Halsey D. Josephson, CLU; New York: Wesley Press, 1960, pp. 154–155.
5. *Insurance Field Magazine,* October 9, 1964, p. 35.
6. *Modern Life Insurance—A Textbook of Income Insurance,* by Robert I. Mehr and Robert W. Osler; revised edition, New York: the Macmillan Co., 1959, p. 611.
7. *Forbes* magazine, December 1, 1966.
8. *Probe,* January 20, 1958.

Chapter 19. Stock Companies— The Astronauts of the Investment World

1. From J. H. Goddard and Company, Inc., Investment Securities, 85 Devonshire Street, Boston, Mass., 1964.
2. Vance Sanders and Company's Capital Exchange Fund, as reported in *National Underwriter,* March 19, 1966, p. 30.
3. *National Underwriter,* October 29, 1966, p. 4.

Chapter 20. G.I. Insurance and the Military Market

1. *National Underwriter,* editorial comment, February 18, 1967, p. 24.
2. *Ibid.*
3. *Business Week* magazine, October 23, 1965, p. 77.
4. Associated Press release, August 12, 1965, as reported in Atlanta *Constitution.*
5. *National Underwriter,* September 3, 1966.
6. *Consumer Reports,* March 1967, p. 163.
7. *National Underwriter,* May 16, 1964.
8. *National Underwriter,* July 16, 1966, pp. 33–34.

Chapter 21. Industrial and Credit Life Insurance

1. *Marketing Life Insurance—Its History in America,* by Dr. J. Owen Stalson; Cambridge: Harvard University Press, 1942, p. 474.
2. "Dirty Deal in Small Loans" by James Ridgeway, *New Republic,* October 8, 1966, pp. 11, 12.

Chapter 22. Social Security

1. *Marketing Life Insurance—Its History in America,* by Dr. J. Owen Stalson; Cambridge: Harvard University Press, 1942, pp. 643–644.
2. *Inspection Service of the Retail Credit Company,* Vol. 48, No. 3, September, 1967, p. 3.

Chapter 23. The Specialty Market

1. *National Underwriter,* November 21, 1964, pp. 1, 28.

Chapter 24. Propaganda

1. Donald F. Barnes, quoted in *National Underwriter,* Nov. 7, 1964.
2. *Ibid.*
3. *Marketing Life Insurance—Its History in America,* by Dr. J. Owen Stalson; Cambridge: Harvard University Press, 1942, p. 146.
4. *Life Association News,* October, 1961, pp. 92 ff.

Chapter 25. Regulation

1. Richard M. Grosten, Los Angeles, California, writing in *Insurance Field Magazine,* October 8, 1965, pp. 25–26.
2. *Probe,* February 6, 1967, p. 4.
3. *Probe,* January 1, 1962.
4. *National Underwriter,* February 22, 1964, p. 23.
5. *The Retail Price Structure in American Life Insurance,* by Dr. Joseph M. Belth; Bloomington: Indiana University Press, 1966, pp. 240–241.
6. *Forbes* magazine, December 1, 1966.

Chapter 26. The Salesman

1. *Insurance Field Magazine,* 'Newsgram,' January 28, 1966.
2. *The Life Insurance Enterprise, 1885–1910,* by Morton Keller, p. 81.
3. *National Underwriter,* March 18, 1967, p. 2.
4. "The Agent's Challenge," *Best's Life News,* November, 1965, p. 41.
5. *Best's Life News,* April, 1966, p. 36.
6. *National Underwriter,* March 27, 1965.
7. *National Underwriter,* editorial comment, February 27, 1965, p. 20.

8. *Probe*, October 8, 1962.
9. *Best's Life News*, October, 1966, pp. 86, 87, "Closing with the Aid of Motion Pictures."
10. *Insurance Field Magazine*, August 13, 1965.
11. *Ibid.*, November 8, 1963.
12. *The Insurance Salesman*, July, 1967.

Chapter 27. Home Office—The Edifice Complex

1. *The Life Insurance Enterprise, 1885–1910*, by Morton Keller; Cambridge: Harvard University Press, 1963, p. 39.
2. *A Family of Thirty Million: The Story of the Metropolitan Life Insurance Company*, by Louis I. Dublin, Ph.D. 3rd Vice President and Statistician; New York, 1943, p. 231.
3. *Best's Life News*, October 1965, p. 88.

Chapter 28. Epilogue

1. *The Great Stewardship: A Story of Life Insurance*, by Albert W. Atwood; New York: Harper & Brothers, 1945, p. 21.
2. *Economic and Social Contributions of Life Insurance to the Nation*, published by the Equitable Life Assurance Society of the United States to commemorate its 100th anniversary. Dr. Bonnell's speech was made on July 28, 1959.

Appendix I

Classifications and Types of "Permanent" Policies

Appendix I

Classifications and Types of "Permanent" Policies

Classifications

1. *Ordinary Life*

This includes all individual life insurance policies in face amounts of more than $1,000. The term is often used as a synonym for "straight" and "whole" life (described below), but this is incorrect usage. Ordinary life, incidentally, includes term insurance along with the so-called "permanent" types.

2. *Group Insurance*

As the name implies, group insurance covers more than one individual under a single policy. For detailed coverage, see Chapter 14. (Some 90 percent of credit life insurance is group insurance.)

3. *Industrial Insurance*

This final general category covers policies issued in amounts of $1,000 and less, the premiums on which are usually collected on a weekly basis. For more detailed discussion, see Chapter 21.

Major Types of So-Called "Permanent" Policies

1. *Whole Life*

This is more a subclassification than a type of policy. It is life insurance for the "whole of life," which mortality tables presently in use set at being to age 100. This does not mean, however, that the policyholder has level protection from the life insurance company for the "whole of life." The protection, or amount that the company is "on the risk," steadily declines toward age 100, at which time (assuming the policyholder is still alive), the policy "endows." The word *endow,* insofar as a life insurance policy is concerned, means simply that the insurer has come entirely off the risk, while at the same time the insured has assumed the total risk. The face amount of a policy, upon endowment, is equal to the Cash Surrender Value.

2. *Straight Life*

As mentioned earlier, "straight," "whole," and "ordinary" are words constantly confused with each other in life insurance. Just as "whole" life is a subclassification under "ordinary," so "straight" life is a type of "whole" life.

Straight life is any policy on which premium payments are payable for the "whole of life," or until the policyholder reaches age 100. Because the premiums are spread over such a span, straight life calls for a lower premium than any other form of permanent insurance.

However, this period includes 35 years past the age of 65— more than an entire generation beyond normal retirement age, and in some cases more than half a century beyond the time that death protection is needed to protect a man's future economic value to his dependents.

3. *Limited-Payment Policies*

This is a form of whole life policy that calls for the payment of premiums for a specific number of years (e.g., 20-Payment Life, etc.), or until a specified age (e.g., Life Paid-Up at Age 55, etc.). All this does is contract the premiums that are to be paid into a shorter span of time. Cash Surrender Values therefore "build" faster, and in so doing, allow the company to come off the risk more rapidly.

The concept of limited-payment, or paid-up, life insurance is entirely misleading, for there is no such thing as a "paid-up" life insurance policy. For detailed discussion of this concept, see Chapter 7.

4. *Endowment Policies*

This is a line of high-cost policies which "endow" (i.e., the Cash Surrender Value becomes the face amount of the policy) at a specified age (such as Endowment at Age 60), or after a specified number of years (such as 20-Year Endowment, etc.). From the standpoint of protection in relation to cost, endowment policies are among the most abusive offerings of the industry.

5. *Annuities*

This is *not* a form of life insurance policy, and is included here only because life insurance companies sell them, and because the companies tie annuities to certain types of policies (see the following Item 6). An annuity is the direct opposite of life insurance in its purpose; that is, an annuity protects against living too long, while life insurance (when used in its true function) protects against dying too soon.

Annuities can be purchased by regular payments over a number of years or by a single payment. Payments from the company to the annuitant may be either for a specified number of years or for life. The amount of these payments is calculated actuarially from the mortality tables.

6. *Retirement-Income Policies*

These are nothing more than "permanent" Cash Surrender Value policies sold for the supposed double purpose of providing protection for dependents in the event of the policyholder's premature death, or providing him with retirement income if he lives. In attempting both in a single package, each endeavor is weakened badly. High Cash Surrender Values have to be generated in order to provide the funds which will be used for the purchase of an annuity at retirement age; therefore, the policy calls for excessively high premiums. The high premiums and high Cash Surrender Value, on the other hand, guarantee that the pure death protection will be greatly watered down, thus crippling the life insurance function.

7. *Family-Income Policy*

This is one of many mongrel policies, combining pure death protection (decreasing-term insurance) with a wad of "straight life." In this and other half-breed policies, the industry refers to the term portion as a "rider," intimating that it got on as something of an afterthought, and should not be considered on a par with the so-called "permanent" portion of the policy. This, as usual, puts the cart before the horse again, for the protection part of the "straight life" itself is pure term insurance. Therefore, if anything about the policy should be called a "rider," it should be the Cash Surrender Value, or "permanent" part—a rider, incidentally, which becomes an increasing burden with the passing years.

The family income policy works like this: It is sold on the basis of a particular "family-income period." For example, on a 20-year family-income policy, should the policyholder die when the contract has been in force 10 years, the term "rider" will supply a set monthly income (generally $10 per $1,000 face amount of the policy) for the remainder of the period—10 years—at which time the face amount of the "straight life" portion is paid to the beneficiaries.

This is very nice—for the company. It allows the company to hang onto and earn interest upon this money until the period ends. Some policies state that the final payment can be made earlier, but when this is done, it is on a "commuted value" basis, which means that the payment is discounted for the years the company is to be denied its use.

Variations on this basic theme vary from company to company, but the principle remains the same.

8. *Modified Life, or Graded-Premium Policies*

This is a widely sold, sneaky little deal, whereby the agent sells his prospect a reasonably priced term policy, and then over the next 3, 5, or 10 years automatically takes it away from him by converting it to a form of "permanent," thereby jacking up the premium payment (*and* the commission).

Avoid it.

9. *Double Protection to Various Ages*

This type of hybrid consists generally of equal parts of term and straight life, which supposedly means that the policy gives "double protection" during the period of the term insurance. It does no such thing, of course, as the "straight life" protection begins to drop the moment any Cash Surrender Value appears on the policy.

Double protection, like any other concoction of the sort, is nothing more than an attempt to make a package that—at first glance—looks attractive. Close inspection is something it cannot successfully undergo.

The names given life insurance policies by the more than 1,700 companies presently operating in the United States are as numerous as the grains of sand on a beach—Jumping Juvenile, Economatic, Signature 25, President's Protective Investment Plan, Gibraltar Series, Golden Accumulator, etc., *ad infinitum, ad nauseam.*

It should always be remembered, that, regardless of the name given or the claim made, the *protection* portion of every life insurance policy ever written is pure term insurance, for the simple reason that term is the *only* kind of life insurance there is.

Appendix II

Decreasing-Term Insurance
Individual Tables
Age 20–55

MALE, AGE 20 (FEMALE, AGE 23)
DECREASING TERM TO AGE 65 (45-YEAR DECREASING TERM)

1	2	3	4	5	6
AT YOUR AGE	BEGINNING OF POLICY YEAR	DEATH PROTECTION	ANNUAL PREMIUM	YEARLY COST PER $1,000	YEAR'S DECREASE IN DEATH PROTECTION
20	1	$100,000	$325.20	$ 3.25	$2,200
21	2	97,800	"	3.33	2,200
22	3	95,600	"	3.40	2,200
23	4	93,400	"	3.48	2,200
24	5	91,200	"	3.57	2,300
25	6	88,900	"	3.66	2,200
26	7	86,700	"	3.75	2,200
27	8	84,500	"	3.85	2,200
28	9	82,300	"	3.95	2,200
29	10	80,100	"	4.06	2,300
30	11	77,800	"	4.18	2,200
31	12	75,600	"	4.30	2,200
32	13	73,400	"	4.43	2,200
33	14	71,200	"	4.57	2,300
34	15	68,900	"	4.72	2,200
35	16	66,700	"	4.88	2,200
36	17	64,500	"	5.04	2,200
37	18	62,300	"	5.22	2,200
38	19	60,100	"	5.41	2,300
39	20	57,800	"	5.63	2,200
40	21	55,600	"	5.85	2,200
41	22	53,400	"	6.09	2,200
42	23	51,200	"	6.35	2,300
43	24	48,900	"	6.65	2,200
44	25	46,700	"	6.96	2,200
45	26	44,500	"	7.31	2,200
46	27	42,300	"	7.69	2,200
47	28	40,100	"	8.11	2,300
48	29	37,800	"	8.60	2,200
49	30	35,600	"	9.13	2,200
50	31	33,400	"	9.74	2,200
51	32	31,200	"	10.42	2,300
52	33	28,900	"	11.25	2,200
53	34	26,700	"	12.18	2,200
54	35	24,500	"	13.27	2,200
55	36	22,300	"	14.58	2,300
56	37	20,000	"	16.26	None
57	38	20,000	"	16.26	None
58	39	20,000	"	16.26	None
59	40	20,000	"	16.26	None
60	41	20,000	322.00†	16.10	None
61	42	20,000	"	16.10	None
62	43	20,000	"	16.10	None
63	44	20,000	"	16.10	None
64*	45	20,000	"	16.10	None
65	46	None*			

* Unless you have decided to convert the remainder as described in text.
† At age 60 waiver of premium no longer effective, premium charge for it no longer payable.

MALE, AGE 21 (FEMALE, AGE 24)
DECREASING TERM TO AGE 65 (44-YEAR DECREASING TERM)

1	2	3	4	5	6
AT YOUR AGE	BEGINNING OF POLICY YEAR	DEATH PROTECTION	ANNUAL PREMIUM	YEARLY COST PER $1,000	YEAR'S DECREASE IN DEATH PROTECTION
21	1	$100,000	$326.00	$ 3.26	$2,200
22	2	97,800	"	3.33	2,300
23	3	95,500	"	3.41	2,300
24	4	93,200	"	3.50	2,300
25	5	90,900	"	3.59	2,300
26	6	88,600	"	3.68	2,300
27	7	86,300	"	3.78	2,300
28	8	84,000	"	3.88	2,200
29	9	81,800	"	3.99	2,300
30	10	79,500	"	4.10	2,300
31	11	77,200	"	4.22	2,300
32	12	74,900	"	4.35	2,300
33	13	72,600	"	4.49	2,300
34	14	70,300	"	4.64	2,300
35	15	68,000	"	4.79	2,200
36	16	65,800	"	4.95	2,300
37	17	63,500	"	5.13	2,300
38	18	61,200	"	5.33	2,300
39	19	58,900	"	5.53	2,300
40	20	56,600	"	5.76	2,300
41	21	54,300	"	6.00	2,300
42	22	52,000	"	6.27	2,200
43	23	49,800	"	6.55	2,300
44	24	47,500	"	6.86	2,300
45	25	45,200	"	7.21	2,300
46	26	42,900	"	7.60	2,300
47	27	40,600	"	8.03	2,300
48	28	38,300	"	8.51	2,300
49	29	36,000	"	9.06	2,200
50	30	33,800	"	9.64	2,300
51	31	31,500	"	10.35	2,300
52	32	29,200	"	11.16	2,300
53	33	26,900	"	12.12	2,300
54	34	24,600	"	13.25	2,300
55	35	22,300	"	14.62	2,300
56	36	20,000	"	16.30	None
57	37	20,000	"	16.30	None
58	38	20,000	"	16.30	None
59	39	20,000	"	16.30	None
60	40	20,000	322.80†	16.14	None
61	41	20,000	"	16.14	None
62	42	20,000	"	16.14	None
63	43	20,000	"	16.14	None
64*	44	20,000	"	16.14	None
65	45	None*			

* Unless you have decided to convert the remainder as described in text.
† At age 60 waiver of premium no longer effective, premium charge for it no longer payable.

MALE, AGE 22 (FEMALE, AGE 25)
DECREASING TERM TO AGE 65 (43-YEAR DECREASING TERM)

1	2	3	4	5	6
					YEAR'S
	BEGINNING			YEARLY	DECREASE
AT YOUR	OF POLICY	DEATH	ANNUAL	COST PER	IN DEATH
AGE	YEAR	PROTECTION	PREMIUM	$1,000	PROTECTION
22	1	$100,000	$327.00	$ 3.27	$2,300
23	2	97,700	"	3.35	2,400
24	3	95,300	"	3.43	2,300
25	4	93,000	"	3.52	2,400
26	5	90,600	"	3.61	2,300
27	6	88,300	"	3.70	2,400
28	7	85,900	"	3.81	2,300
29	8	83,600	"	3.91	2,400
30	9	81,200	"	4.03	2,300
31	10	78,900	"	4.14	2,400
32	11	76,500	"	4.27	2,300
33	12	74,200	"	4.41	2,400
34	13	71,800	"	4.55	2,300
35	14	69,500	"	4.71	2,400
36	15	67,100	"	4.87	2,300
37	16	64,800	"	5.05	2,400
38	17	62,400	"	5.24	2,400
39	18	60,000	"	5.45	2,300
40	19	57,700	"	5.67	2,400
41	20	55,300	"	5.91	2,300
42	21	53,000	"	6.17	2,400
43	22	50,600	"	6.46	2,300
44	23	48,300	"	6.77	2,400
45	24	45,900	"	7.12	2,300
46	25	43,600	"	7.50	2,400
47	26	41,200	"	7.94	2,300
48	27	38,900	"	8.41	2,400
49	28	36,500	"	8.96	2,300
50	29	34,200	"	9.56	2,400
51	30	31,800	"	10.28	2,300
52	31	29,500	"	11.08	2,400
53	32	27,100	"	12.07	2,300
54	33	24,800	"	13.19	2,400
55	34	22,400	"	14.60	2,400
56	35	20,000	"	16.35	None
57	36	20,000	"	16.35	None
58	37	20,000	"	16.35	None
59	38	20,000	"	16.35	None
60	39	20,000	323.80†	16.19	None
61	40	20,000	"	16.19	None
62	41	20,000	"	16.19	None
63	42	20,000	"	16.19	None
64*	43	20,000	"	16.19	None
65	44	None*			

* Unless you have decided to convert the remainder as described in text.
† At age 60 waiver of premium no longer effective, premium charge for it no longer payable.

MALE, AGE 23 (FEMALE, AGE 26)
DECREASING TERM TO AGE 65 (42-YEAR DECREASING TERM)

1	2	3	4	5	6
AT YOUR AGE	BEGINNING OF POLICY YEAR	DEATH PROTECTION	ANNUAL PREMIUM	YEARLY COST PER $1,000	YEAR'S DECREASE IN DEATH PROTECTION
23	1	$100,000	$328.00	$ 3.28	$2,300
24	2	97,700	"	3.36	2,400
25	3	95,300	"	3.44	2,300
26	4	93,000	"	3.53	2,400
27	5	90,600	"	3.62	2,300
28	6	88,300	"	3.71	2,400
29	7	85,900	"	3.82	2,300
30	8	83,600	"	3.92	2,400
31	9	81,200	"	4.04	2,300
32	10	78,900	"	4.16	2,400
33	11	76,500	"	4.29	2,300
34	12	74,200	"	4.42	2,400
35	13	71,800	"	4.57	2,300
36	14	69,500	"	4.72	2,400
37	15	67,100	"	4.89	2,300
38	16	64,800	"	5.06	2,400
39	17	62,400	"	5.26	2,400
40	18	60,000	"	5.47	2,300
41	19	57,700	"	5.68	2,400
42	20	55,300	"	5.93	2,300
43	21	53,000	"	6.19	2,400
44	22	50,600	"	6.48	2,300
45	23	48,300	"	6.79	2,400
46	24	45,900	"	7.15	2,300
47	25	43,600	"	7.52	2,400
48	26	41,200	"	7.96	2,300
49	27	38,900	"	8.43	2,400
50	28	36,500	"	8.99	2,300
51	29	34,200	"	9.59	2,400
52	30	31,800	"	10.31	2,300
53	31	29,500	"	11.12	2,400
54	32	27,100	"	12.10	2,300
55	33	24,800	"	13.23	2,400
56	34	22,400	"	14.64	2,400
57	35	20,000	"	16.40	None
58	36	20,000	"	16.40	None
59	37	20,000	"	16.40	None
60	38	20,000	324.80†	16.24	None
61	39	20,000	"	16.24	None
62	40	20,000	"	16.24	None
63	41	20,000	"	16.24	None
64*	42	20,000	"	16.24	None
65	43	None*			

* Unless you have decided to convert the remainder as described in text.
† At age 60 waiver of premium no longer effective, premium charge for it no longer payable.

MALE, AGE 24 (FEMALE, AGE 27)
DECREASING TERM TO AGE 65 (41-YEAR DECREASING TERM)

1 AT YOUR AGE	2 BEGINNING OF POLICY YEAR	3 DEATH PROTECTION	4 ANNUAL PREMIUM	5 YEARLY COST PER $1,000	6 YEAR'S DECREASE IN DEATH PROTECTION
24	1	$100,000	$329.20	$ 3.29	$2,400
25	2	97,600	"	3.37	2,400
26	3	95,200	"	3.46	2,400
27	4	92,800	"	3.55	2,400
28	5	90,400	"	3.64	2,500
29	6	87,900	"	3.75	2,400
30	7	85,500	"	3.85	2,400
31	8	83,100	"	3.96	2,400
32	9	80,700	"	4.08	2,500
33	10	78,200	"	4.21	2,400
34	11	75,800	"	4.34	2,400
35	12	73,400	"	4.49	2,400
36	13	71,000	"	4.64	2,500
37	14	68,500	"	4.81	2,400
38	15	66,100	"	4.98	2,400
39	16	63,700	"	5.17	2,400
40	17	61,300	"	5.37	2,500
41	18	58,800	"	5.60	2,400
42	19	56,400	"	5.84	2,400
43	20	54,000	"	6.10	2,400
44	21	51,600	"	6.38	2,500
45	22	49,100	"	6.70	2,400
46	23	46,700	"	7.05	2,400
47	24	44,300	"	7.43	2,400
48	25	41,900	"	7.86	2,500
49	26	39,400	"	8.36	2,400
50	27	37,000	"	8.90	2,400
51	28	34,600	"	9.51	2,400
52	29	32,200	"	10.22	2,400
53	30	29,800	"	11.05	2,500
54	31	27,300	"	12.06	2,400
55	32	24,900	"	13.22	2,400
56	33	22,500	"	14.63	2,500
57	34	20,000	"	16.46	None
58	35	20,000	"	16.46	None
59	36	20,000	"	16.46	None
60	37	20,000	325.80†	16.29	None
61	38	20,000	"	16.29	None
62	39	20,000	"	16.29	None
63	40	20,000	"	16.29	None
64*	41	20,000	"	16.29	None
65	42	None*			

* Unless you have decided to convert the remainder as described in text.
† At age 60 waiver of premium no longer effective, premium charge for it no longer payable.

MALE, AGE 25 (FEMALE, AGE 28)
DECREASING TERM TO AGE 65 (40-YEAR DECREASING TERM)

1	2	3	4	5	6
AT YOUR AGE	BEGINNING OF POLICY YEAR	DEATH PROTECTION	ANNUAL PREMIUM	YEARLY COST PER $1,000	YEAR'S DECREASE IN DEATH PROTECTION
25	1	$100,000	$330.40	$ 3.30	$2,500
26	2	97,500	"	3.39	2,500
27	3	95,000	"	3.48	2,500
28	4	92,500	"	3.57	2,500
29	5	90,000	"	3.67	2,500
30	6	87,500	"	3.78	2,500
31	7	85,000	"	3.89	2,500
32	8	82,500	"	4.00	2,500
33	9	80,000	"	4.13	2,500
34	10	77,500	"	4.26	2,500
35	11	75,000	"	4.41	2,500
36	12	72,500	"	4.56	2,500
37	13	70,000	"	4.72	2,500
38	14	67,500	"	4.89	2,500
39	15	65,000	"	5.08	2,500
40	16	62,500	"	5.29	2,500
41	17	60,000	"	5.51	2,500
42	18	57,500	"	5.75	2,500
43	19	55,000	"	6.01	2,500
44	20	52,500	"	6.29	2,500
45	21	50,000	"	6.61	2,500
46	22	47,500	"	6.96	2,500
47	23	45,000	"	7.34	2,500
48	24	42,500	"	7.77	2,500
49	25	40,000	"	8.26	2,500
50	26	37,500	"	8.81	2,500
51	27	35,000	"	9.44	2,500
52	28	32,500	"	10.17	2,500
53	29	30,000	"	11.01	2,500
54	30	27,500	"	12.01	2,500
55	31	25,000	"	13.22	2,500
56	32	22,500	"	14.68	2,500
57	33	20,000	"	16.52	None
58	34	20,000	"	16.52	None
59	35	20,000	"	16.52	None
60	36	20,000	326.80†	16.34	None
61	37	20,000	"	16.34	None
62	38	20,000	"	16.34	None
63	39	20,000	"	16.34	None
64*	40	20,000	"	16.34	None
65	41	None*			

* Unless you have decided to convert the remainder as described in text.
† At age 60 waiver of premium no longer effective, premium charge for it no longer payable.

MALE, AGE 26 (FEMALE, AGE 29)
DECREASING TERM TO AGE 65 (39-YEAR DECREASING TERM)

1	2	3	4	5	6
AT YOUR AGE	BEGINNING OF POLICY YEAR	DEATH PROTECTION	ANNUAL PREMIUM	YEARLY COST PER $1,000	YEAR'S DECREASE IN DEATH PROTECTION
26	1	$100,000	$332.40	$ 3.32	$2,500
27	2	97,500	"	3.41	2,600
28	3	94,900	"	3.50	2,600
29	4	92,300	"	3.60	2,600
30	5	89,700	"	3.71	2,600
31	6	87,100	"	3.82	2,500
32	7	84,600	"	3.93	2,600
33	8	82,000	"	4.05	2,600
34	9	79,400	"	4.19	2,600
35	10	76,800	"	4.33	2,600
36	11	74,200	"	4.48	2,500
37	12	71,700	"	4.64	2,600
38	13	69,100	"	4.81	2,600
39	14	66,500	"	5.00	2,600
40	15	63,900	"	5.20	2,600
41	16	61,300	"	5.42	2,500
42	17	58,800	"	5.65	2,600
43	18	56,200	"	5.91	2,600
44	19	53,600	"	6.20	2,600
45	20	51,000	"	6.52	2,600
46	21	48,400	"	6.87	2,600
47	22	45,800	"	7.26	2,500
48	23	43,300	"	7.68	2,600
49	24	40,700	"	8.17	2,600
50	25	38,100	"	8.72	2,600
51	26	35,500	"	9.36	2,600
52	27	32,900	"	10.10	2,500
53	28	30,400	"	10.93	2,600
54	29	27,800	"	11.96	2,600
55	30	25,200	"	13.19	2,600
56	31	22,600	"	14.71	2,600
57	32	20,000	"	16.62	None
58	33	20,000	"	16.62	None
59	34	20,000	"	16.62	None
60	35	20,000	328.60†	16.43	None
61	36	20,000	"	16.43	None
62	37	20,000	"	16.43	None
63	38	20,000	"	16.43	None
64*	39	20,000	"	16.43	None
65	40	None*			

* Unless you have decided to convert the remainder as described in text.
† At age 60 waiver of premium no longer effective, premium charge for it no longer payable.

MALE, AGE 27 (FEMALE, AGE 30)
DECREASING TERM TO AGE 65 (38-YEAR DECREASING TERM)

1	2	3	4	5	6
AT YOUR AGE	BEGINNING OF POLICY YEAR	DEATH PROTECTION	ANNUAL PREMIUM	YEARLY COST PER $1,000	YEAR'S DECREASE IN DEATH PROTECTION
27	1	$100,000	$334.40	$ 3.34	$2,600
28	2	97,400	"	3.43	2,700
29	3	94,700	"	3.53	2,700
30	4	92,000	"	3.63	2,600
31	5	89,400	"	3.74	2,700
32	6	86,700	"	3.86	2,700
33	7	84,000	"	3.98	2,600
34	8	81,400	"	4.11	2,700
35	9	78,700	"	4.25	2,700
36	10	76,000	"	4.40	2,600
37	11	73,400	"	4.56	2,700
38	12	70,700	"	4.73	2,700
39	13	68,000	"	4.92	2,600
40	14	65,400	"	5.11	2,700
41	15	62,700	"	5.33	2,700
42	16	60,000	"	5.57	2,600
43	17	57,400	"	5.83	2,700
44	18	54,700	"	6.11	2,700
45	19	52,000	"	6.43	2,600
46	20	49,400	"	6.77	2,700
47	21	46,700	"	7.16	2,700
48	22	44,000	"	7.60	2,600
49	23	41,400	"	8.08	2,700
50	24	38,700	"	8.64	2,700
51	25	36,000	"	9.29	2,600
52	26	33,400	"	10.01	2,700
53	27	30,700	"	10.89	2,700
54	28	28,000	"	11.94	2,600
55	29	25,400	"	13.17	2,700
56	30	22,700	"	14.73	2,700
57	31	20,000	"	16.72	None
58	32	20,000	"	16.72	None
59	33	20,000	"	16.72	None
60	34	20,000	330.20†	16.51	None
61	35	20,000	"	16.51	None
62	36	20,000	"	16.51	None
63	37	20,000	"	16.51	None
64*	38	20,000	"	16.51	None
65	39	None*			

* Unless you have decided to convert the remainder as described in text.
† At age 60 waiver of premium no longer effective, premium charge for it no longer payable.

MALE, AGE 28 (FEMALE, AGE 31)
DECREASING TERM TO AGE 65 (37-YEAR DECREASING TERM)

1	2	3	4	5	6
AT YOUR AGE	BEGINNING OF POLICY YEAR	DEATH PROTECTION	ANNUAL PREMIUM	YEARLY COST PER $1,000	YEAR'S DECREASE IN DEATH PROTECTION
28	1	$100,000	$336.40	$ 3.36	$2,600
29	2	97,400	"	3.45	2,700
30	3	94,700	"	3.55	2,700
31	4	92,000	"	3.66	2,600
32	5	89,400	"	3.76	2,700
33	6	86,700	"	3.88	2,700
34	7	84,000	"	4.00	2,600
35	8	81,400	"	4.13	2,700
36	9	78,700	"	4.27	2,700
37	10	76,000	"	4.43	2,600
38	11	73,400	"	4.58	2,700
39	12	70,700	"	4.76	2,700
40	13	68,000	"	4.95	2,600
41	14	65,400	"	5.14	2,700
42	15	62,700	"	5.37	2,700
43	16	60,000	"	5.61	2,600
44	17	57,400	"	5.86	2,700
45	18	54,700	"	6.15	2,700
46	19	52,000	"	6.47	2,600
47	20	49,400	"	6.81	2,700
48	21	46,700	"	7.20	2,700
49	22	44,000	"	7.65	2,600
50	23	41,400	"	8.13	2,700
51	24	38,700	"	8.69	2,700
52	25	36,000	"	9.34	2,600
53	26	33,400	"	10.07	2,700
54	27	30,700	"	10.96	2,700
55	28	28,000	"	12.01	2,600
56	29	25,400	"	13.24	2,700
57	30	22,700	"	14.82	2,700
58	31	20,000	"	16.82	None
59	32	20,000	"	16.82	None
60	33	20,000	331.80†	16.59	None
61	34	20,000	"	16.59	None
62	35	20,000	"	16.59	None
63	36	20,000	"	16.59	None
64*	37	20,000	"	16.59	None
65	38	None*			

* Unless you have decided to convert the remainder as described in text.
† At age 60 waiver of premium no longer effective, premium charge for it no longer payable.

MALE, AGE 29 (FEMALE, AGE 32)
DECREASING TERM TO AGE 65 (36-YEAR DECREASING TERM)

1	2	3	4	5	6
AT YOUR AGE	BEGINNING OF POLICY YEAR	DEATH PROTECTION	ANNUAL PREMIUM	YEARLY COST PER $1,000	YEAR'S DECREASE IN DEATH PROTECTION
29	1	$100,000	$338.60	$ 3.39	$2,700
30	2	97,300	"	3.48	2,800
31	3	94,500	"	3.58	2,700
32	4	91,800	"	3.69	2,800
33	5	89,000	"	3.80	2,700
34	6	86,300	"	3.92	2,800
35	7	83,500	"	4.06	2,800
36	8	80,700	"	4.20	2,700
37	9	78,000	"	4.34	2,800
38	10	75,200	"	4.50	2,700
39	11	72,500	"	4.67	2,800
40	12	69,700	"	4.86	2,800
41	13	66,900	"	5.06	2,700
42	14	64,200	"	5.27	2,800
43	15	61,400	"	5.51	2,700
44	16	58,700	"	5.77	2,800
45	17	55,900	"	6.06	2,800
46	18	53,100	"	6.38	2,700
47	19	50,400	"	6.72	2,800
48	20	47,600	"	7.11	2,700
49	21	44,900	"	7.54	2,800
50	22	42,100	"	8.04	2,700
51	23	39,400	"	8.59	2,800
52	24	36,600	"	9.25	2,800
53	25	33,800	"	10.02	2,700
54	26	31,100	"	10.89	2,800
55	27	28,300	"	11.96	2,700
56	28	25,600	"	13.23	2,800
57	29	22,800	"	14.85	2,800
58	30	20,000	"	16.93	None
59	31	20,000		16.93	None
60	32	20,000	333.60†	16.68	None
61	33	20,000	"	16.68	None
62	34	20,000	"	16.68	None
63	35	20,000	"	16.68	None
64*	36	20,000	"	16.68	None
65	37	None*			

* Unless you have decided to convert the remainder as described in text.
† At age 60 waiver of premium no longer effective, premium charge for it no longer payable.

MALE, AGE 30 (FEMALE, AGE 33)
DECREASING TERM TO AGE 65 (35-YEAR DECREASING TERM)

1	2	3	4	5	6
AT YOUR AGE	BEGINNING OF POLICY YEAR	DEATH PROTECTION	ANNUAL PREMIUM	YEARLY COST PER $1,000	YEAR'S DECREASE IN DEATH PROTECTION
30	1	$100,000	$340.60	$ 3.41	$2,800
31	2	97,200	"	3.50	2,900
32	3	94,300	"	3.61	2,800
33	4	91,500	"	3.72	2,900
34	5	88,600	"	3.84	2,800
35	6	85,800	"	3.97	2,900
36	7	82,900	"	4.11	2,800
37	8	80,100	"	4.25	2,900
38	9	77,200	"	4.41	2,900
39	10	74,300	"	4.58	2,800
40	11	71,500	"	4.76	2,900
41	12	68,600	"	4.97	2,800
42	13	65,800	"	5.18	2,900
43	14	62,900	"	5.41	2,800
44	15	60,100	"	5.67	2,900
45	16	57,200	"	5.95	2,900
46	17	54,300	"	6.27	2,800
47	18	51,500	"	6.61	2,900
48	19	48,600	"	7.01	2,800
49	20	45,800	"	7.44	2,900
50	21	42,900	"	7.94	2,800
51	22	40,100	"	8.49	2,900
52	23	37,200	"	9.16	2,900
53	24	34,300	"	9.93	2,800
54	25	31,500	"	10.81	2,900
55	26	28,600	"	11.91	2,800
56	27	25,800	"	13.20	2,900
57	28	22,900	"	14.87	2,900
58	29	20,000	"	17.03	None
59	30	20,000	"	17.03	None
60	31	20,000	335.20†	16.76	None
61	32	20,000	"	16.76	None
62	33	20,000	"	16.76	None
63	34	20,000	"	16.76	None
64*	35	20,000	"	16.76	None
65	36	None*			

* Unless you have decided to convert the remainder as described in text.
† At age 60 waiver of premium no longer effective, premium charge for it no longer payable.

MALE, AGE 31 (FEMALE, AGE 34)
DECREASING TERM TO AGE 65 (34-YEAR DECREASING TERM)

1	2	3	4	5	6
AT YOUR AGE	BEGINNING OF POLICY YEAR	DEATH PROTECTION	ANNUAL PREMIUM	YEARLY COST PER $1,000	YEAR'S DECREASE IN DEATH PROTECTION
31	1	$100,000	$347.40	$ 3.47	$2,900
32	2	97,100	"	3.58	3,000
33	3	94,100	"	3.69	2,900
34	4	91,200	"	3.81	3,000
35	5	88,200	"	3.94	3,000
36	6	85,200	"	4.08	2,900
37	7	82,300	"	4.22	3,000
38	8	79,300	"	4.38	3,000
39	9	76,300	"	4.55	2,900
40	10	73,400	"	4.73	3,000
41	11	70,400	"	4.93	2,900
42	12	67,500	"	5.15	3,000
43	13	64,500	"	5.39	3,000
44	14	61,500	"	5.65	2,900
45	15	58,600	"	5.93	3,000
46	16	55,600	"	6.25	3,000
47	17	52,600	"	6.60	2,900
48	18	49,700	"	6.99	3,000
49	19	46,700	"	7.44	2,900
50	20	43,800	"	7.93	3,000
51	21	40,800	"	8.51	3,000
52	22	37,800	"	9.19	2,900
53	23	34,900	"	9.95	3,000
54	24	31,900	"	10.89	3,000
55	25	28,900	"	12.02	2,900
56	26	26,000	"	13.36	3,000
57	27	23,000	"	15.10	3,000
58	28	20,000	"	17.37	None
59	29	20,000	"	17.37	None
60	30	20,000	341.80†	17.09	None
61	31	20,000	"	17.09	None
62	32	20,000	"	17.09	None
63	33	20,000	"	17.09	None
64*	34	20,000	"	17.09	None
65	35	None*			

* Unless you have decided to convert the remainder as described in text.
† At age 60 waiver of premium no longer effective, premium charge for it no longer payable.

MALE, AGE 32 (FEMALE, AGE 35)
DECREASING TERM TO AGE 65 (33-YEAR DECREASING TERM)

1	2	3	4	5	6
AT YOUR AGE	BEGINNING OF POLICY YEAR	DEATH PROTECTION	ANNUAL PREMIUM	YEARLY COST PER $1,000	YEAR'S DECREASE IN DEATH PROTECTION
32	1	$100,000	$355.80	$ 3.56	$3,000
33	2	97,000	"	3.67	3,100
34	3	93,900	"	3.79	3,100
35	4	90,800	"	3.92	3,100
36	5	87,700	"	4.06	3,000
37	6	84,700	"	4.20	3,100
38	7	81,600	"	4.36	3,100
39	8	78,500	"	4.53	3,100
40	9	75,400	"	4.72	3,000
41	10	72,400	"	4.91	3,100
42	11	69,300	"	5.13	3,100
43	12	66,200	"	5.37	3,100
44	13	63,100	"	5.64	3,100
45	14	60,000	"	5.93	3,000
46	15	57,000	"	6.24	3,100
47	16	53,900	"	6.60	3,100
48	17	50,800	"	7.00	3,100
49	18	47,700	"	7.46	3,000
50	19	44,700	"	7.96	3,100
51	20	41,600	"	8.55	3,100
52	21	38,500	"	9.24	3,100
53	22	35,400	"	10.05	3,000
54	23	32,400	"	10.98	3,100
55	24	29,300	"	12.14	3,100
56	25	26,200	"	13.58	3,100
57	26	23,100	"	15.40	3,100
58	27	20,000	"	17.79	None
59	28	20,000	"	17.79	None
60	29	20,000	349.80†	17.49	None
61	30	20,000	"	17.49	None
62	31	20,000	"	17.49	None
63	32	20,000	"	17.49	None
64*	33	20,000	"	17.49	None
65	34	None*			

* Unless you have decided to convert the remainder as described in text.
† At age 60 waiver of premium no longer effective, premium charge for it no longer payable.

MALE, AGE 33 (FEMALE, AGE 36)
DECREASING TERM TO AGE 65 (32-YEAR DECREASING TERM)

1	2	3	4	5	6
AT YOUR AGE	BEGINNING OF POLICY YEAR	DEATH PROTECTION	ANNUAL PREMIUM	YEARLY COST PER $1,000	YEAR'S DECREASE IN DEATH PROTECTION
33	1	$100,000	$366.20	$ 3.66	$3,000
34	2	97,000	"	3.78	3,100
35	3	93,900	"	3.90	3,100
36	4	90,800	"	4.03	3,100
37	5	87,700	"	4.18	3,000
38	6	84,700	"	4.32	3,100
39	7	81,600	"	4.49	3,100
40	8	78,500	"	4.66	3,100
41	9	75,400	"	4.86	3,000
42	10	72,400	"	5.06	3,100
43	11	69,300	"	5.28	3,100
44	12	66,200	"	5.53	3,100
45	13	63,100	"	5.80	3,100
46	14	60,000	"	6.10	3,000
47	15	57,000	"	6.42	3,100
48	16	53,900	"	6.79	3,100
49	17	50,800	"	7.21	3,100
50	18	47,700	"	7.68	3,000
51	19	44,700	"	8.19	3,100
52	20	41,600	"	8.80	3,100
53	21	38,500	"	9.51	3,100
54	22	35,400	"	10.34	3,000
55	23	32,400	"	11.30	3,100
56	24	29,300	"	12.50	3,100
57	25	26,200	"	13.98	3,100
58	26	23,100	"	15.85	3,100
59	27	20,000	"	18.31	None
60	28	20,000	359.80†	17.99	None
61	29	20,000	"	17.99	None
62	30	20,000	"	17.99	None
63	31	20,000	"	17.99	None
64*	32	20,000	"	17.99	None
65	33	None*			

* Unless you have decided to convert the remainder as described in text.
† At age 60 waiver of premium no longer effective, premium charge for it no longer payable.

MALE, AGE 34 (FEMALE, AGE 37)
DECREASING TERM TO AGE 65 (31-YEAR DECREASING TERM)

1	2	3	4	5	6
AT YOUR AGE	BEGINNING OF POLICY YEAR	DEATH PROTECTION	ANNUAL PREMIUM	YEARLY COST PER $1,000	YEAR'S DECREASE IN DEATH PROTECTION
34	1	$100,000	$378.80	$ 3.79	$3,200
35	2	96,800	"	3.91	3,200
36	3	93,600	"	4.05	3,200
37	4	90,400	"	4.19	3,200
38	5	87,200	"	4.34	3,200
39	6	84,000	"	4.51	3,200
40	7	80,800	"	4.69	3,200
41	8	77,600	"	4.88	3,200
42	9	74,400	"	5.09	3,200
43	10	71,200	"	5.32	3,200
44	11	68,000	"	5.57	3,200
45	12	64,800	"	5.85	3,200
46	13	61,600	"	6.15	3,200
47	14	58,400	"	6.49	3,200
48	15	55,200	"	6.86	3,200
49	16	52,000	"	7.28	3,200
50	17	48,800	"	7.76	3,200
51	18	45,600	"	8.31	3,200
52	19	42,400	"	8.93	3,200
53	20	39,200	"	9.66	3,200
54	21	36,000	"	10.52	3,200
55	22	32,800	"	11.55	3,200
56	23	29,600	"	12.80	3,200
57	24	26,400	"	14.35	3,200
58	25	23,200	"	16.33	3.200
59	26	20,000	"	18.94	None
60	27	20,000	371.80†	18.59	None
61	28	20,000	"	18.59	None
62	29	20,000	"	18.59	None
63	30	20,000	"	18.59	None
64*	31	20,000	"	18.59	None
65	32	None*			

* Unless you have decided to convert the remainder as described in text.
† At age 60 waiver of premium no longer effective, premium charge for it no longer payable.

MALE, AGE 35 (FEMALE, AGE 38)
DECREASING TERM TO AGE 65 (30-YEAR DECREASING TERM)

1	2	3	4	5	6
AT YOUR AGE	BEGINNING OF POLICY YEAR	DEATH PROTECTION	ANNUAL PREMIUM	YEARLY COST PER $1,000	YEAR'S DECREASE IN DEATH PROTECTION
35	1	$100,000	$393.80	$ 3.94	$3,300
36	2	96,700	"	4.07	3,300
37	3	93,400	"	4.22	3,400
38	4	90,000	"	4.38	3,300
39	5	86,700	"	4.54	3,300
40	6	83,400	"	4.72	3,400
41	7	80,000	"	4.92	3,300
42	8	76,700	"	5.13	3,300
43	9	73,400	"	5.37	3,400
44	10	70,000	"	5.63	3,300
45	11	66,700	"	5.90	3,300
46	12	63,400	"	6.21	3,400
47	13	60,000	"	6.56	3,300
48	14	56,700	"	6.95	3,300
49	15	53,400	"	7.37	3,400
50	16	50,000	"	7.88	3,300
51	17	46,700	"	8.43	3,300
52	18	43,400	"	9.07	3,400
53	19	40,000	"	9.85	3,300
54	20	36,700	"	10.73	3,300
55	21	33,400	"	11.79	3,400
56	22	30,000	"	13.13	3,300
57	23	26,700	"	14.75	3,300
58	24	23,400	"	16.83	3,400
59	25	20,000	"	19.69	None
60	26	20,000	386.20†	19.31	None
61	27	20,000	"	19.31	None
62	28	20,000	"	19.31	None
63	29	20,000	"	19.31	None
64*	30	20,000	"	19.31	None
65	31	None*			

* Unless you have decided to convert the remainder as described in text.
† At age 60 waiver of premium no longer effective, premium charge for it no longer payable.

MALE, AGE 36 (FEMALE, AGE 39)
DECREASING TERM TO AGE 65 (29-YEAR DECREASING TERM)

1	2	3	4	5	6
AT YOUR AGE	BEGINNING OF POLICY YEAR	DEATH PROTECTION	ANNUAL PREMIUM	YEARLY COST PER $1,000	YEAR'S DECREASE IN DEATH PROTECTION
36	1	$100,000	$411.60	$ 4.12	$3,400
37	2	96,600	"	4.26	3,500
38	3	93,100	"	4.42	3,500
39	4	89,600	"	4.59	3,500
40	5	86,100	"	4.78	3,400
41	6	82,700	"	4.98	3,500
42	7	79,200	"	5.20	3,500
43	8	75,700	"	5.44	3,500
44	9	72,200	"	5.70	3,500
45	10	68,700	"	5.99	3,400
46	11	65,300	"	6.30	3,500
47	12	61,800	"	6.66	3,500
48	13	58,300	"	7.06	3,500
49	14	54,800	"	7.51	3,400
50	15	51,400	"	8.01	3,500
51	16	47,900	"	8.59	3,500
52	17	44,400	"	9.27	3,500
53	18	40,900	"	10.06	3,500
54	19	37,400	"	11.01	3,400
55	20	34,000	"	12.11	3,500
56	21	30,500	"	13.50	3,500
57	22	27,000	"	15.24	3,500
58	23	23,500	"	17.51	3,500
59	24	20,000	"	20.58	None
60	25	20,000	402.80†	20.14	None
61	26	20,000	"	20.14	None
62	27	20,000	"	20.14	None
63	28	20,000	"	20.14	None
64*	29	20,000	"	20.14	None
65	30	None*			

* Unless you have decided to convert the remainder as described in text.
† At age 60 waiver of premium no longer effective, premium charge for it no longer payable.

MALE, AGE 37 (FEMALE, AGE 40)
DECREASING TERM TO AGE 65 (28-YEAR DECREASING TERM)

1	2	3	4	5	6
					YEAR'S
	BEGINNING			YEARLY	DECREASE
AT YOUR	OF POLICY	DEATH	ANNUAL	COST PER	IN DEATH
AGE	YEAR	PROTECTION	PREMIUM	$1,000	PROTECTION
37	1	$100,000	$431.60	$ 4.32	$3,600
38	2	96,400	"	4.48	3,600
39	3	92,800	"	4.65	3,700
40	4	89,100	"	4.84	3,600
41	5	85,500	"	5.05	3,600
42	6	81,900	"	5.27	3,700
43	7	78,200	"	5.52	3,600
44	8	74,600	"	5.79	3,600
45	9	71,000	"	6.08	3,700
46	10	67,300	"	6.41	3,600
47	11	63,700	"	6.78	3,600
48	12	60,100	"	7.18	3,700
49	13	56,400	"	7.65	3,600
50	14	52,800	"	8.17	3,600
51	15	49,200	"	8.77	3,700
52	16	45,500	"	9.49	3,600
53	17	41,900	"	10.30	3,600
54	18	38,300	"	11.27	3,700
55	19	34,600	"	12.47	3,600
56	20	31,000	"	13.92	3,700
57	21	27,300	"	15.81	3,600
58	22	23,700	"	18.21	3,700
59	23	20,000	"	21.58	None
60	24	20,000	421.60†	21.08	None
61	25	20,000	"	21.08	None
62	26	20,000	"	21.08	None
63	27	20,000	"	21.08	None
64*	28	20,000	"	21.08	None
65	29	None*			

* Unless you have decided to convert the remainder as described in text.
† At age 60 waiver of premium no longer effective, premium charge for it no longer payable.

MALE, AGE 38 (FEMALE, AGE 41)
DECREASING TERM TO AGE 65 (27-YEAR DECREASING TERM)

1	2	3	4	5	6
AT YOUR AGE	BEGINNING OF POLICY YEAR	DEATH PROTECTION	ANNUAL PREMIUM	YEARLY COST PER $1,000	YEAR'S DECREASE IN DEATH PROTECTION
38	1	$100,000	$454.20	$ 4.54	$3,600
39	2	96,400	"	4.71	3,600
40	3	92,800	"	4.89	3,700
41	4	89,100	"	5.10	3,600
42	5	85,500	"	5.31	3,600
43	6	81,900	"	5.55	3,700
44	7	78,200	"	5.81	3,600
45	8	74,600	"	6.09	3,600
46	9	71,000	"	6.40	3,700
47	10	67,300	"	6.75	3,600
48	11	63,700	"	7.13	3,600
49	12	60,100	"	7.56	3,700
50	13	56,400	"	8.05	3,600
51	14	52,800	"	8.60	3,600
52	15	49,200	"	9.23	3,700
53	16	45,500	"	9.98	3,600
54	17	41,900	"	10.84	3,600
55	18	38,300	"	11.86	3,700
56	19	34,600	"	13.13	3,600
57	20	31,000	"	14.65	3,700
58	21	27,300	"	16.64	3,600
59	22	23,700	"	19.16	3,700
60	23	20,000	442.80†	22.14	None
61	24	20,000	"	22.14	None
62	25	20,000	"	22.14	None
63	26	20,000	"	22.14	None
64*	27	20,000	"	22.14	None
65	28	None*			

* Unless you have decided to convert the remainder as described in text.
† At age 60 waiver of premium no longer effective, premium charge for it no longer payable.

MALE, AGE 39 (FEMALE, AGE 42)
DECREASING TERM TO AGE 65 (26-YEAR DECREASING TERM)

1	2	3	4	5	6
AT YOUR AGE	BEGINNING OF POLICY YEAR	DEATH PROTECTION	ANNUAL PREMIUM	YEARLY COST PER $1,000	YEAR'S DECREASE IN DEATH PROTECTION
39	1	$100,000	$479.60	$ 4.80	$3,800
40	2	96,200	"	4.99	3,800
41	3	92,400	"	5.19	3,800
42	4	88,600	"	5.41	3,800
43	5	84,800	"	5.66	3,800
44	6	81,000	"	5.92	3,800
45	7	77,200	"	6.21	3,800
46	8	73,400	"	6.53	3,800
47	9	69,600	"	6.89	3,800
48	10	65,800	"	7.29	3,900
49	11	61,900	"	7.75	3,800
50	12	58,100	"	8.25	3,800
51	13	54,300	"	8.83	3,800
52	14	50,500	"	9.50	3,800
53	15	46,700	"	10.27	3,800
54	16	42,900	"	11.18	3,800
55	17	39,100	"	12.27	3,800
56	18	35,300	"	13.59	3,800
57	19	31,500	"	15.23	3,800
58	20	27,700	"	17.31	3,900
59	21	23,800	"	20.15	3,800
60	22	20,000	466.80†	23.34	None
61	23	20,000	"	23.34	None
62	24	20,000	"	23.34	None
63	25	20,000	"	23.34	None
64*	26	20,000	"	23.34	None
65	27	None*			

* Unless you have decided to convert the remainder as described in text.
† At age 60 waiver of premium no longer effective, premium charge for it no longer payable.

MALE, AGE 40 (FEMALE, AGE 43)
DECREASING TERM TO AGE 65 (25-YEAR DECREASING TERM)

1	2	3	4	5	6
AT YOUR AGE	BEGINNING OF POLICY YEAR	DEATH PROTECTION	ANNUAL PREMIUM	YEARLY COST PER $1,000	YEAR'S DECREASE IN DEATH PROTECTION
40	1	$100,000	$508.40	$ 5.08	$4,000
41	2	96,000	"	5.30	4,000
42	3	92,000	"	5.53	4,000
43	4	88,000	"	5.78	4,000
44	5	84,000	"	6.05	4,000
45	6	80,000	"	6.36	4,000
46	7	76,000	"	6.69	4,000
47	8	72,000	"	7.06	4,000
48	9	68,000	"	7.48	4,000
49	10	64,000	"	7.94	4,000
50	11	60,000	"	8.47	4,000
51	12	56,000	"	9.08	4,000
52	13	52,000	"	9.78	4,000
53	14	48,000	"	10.59	4,000
54	15	44,000	"	11.55	4,000
55	16	40,000	"	12.71	4,000
56	17	36,000	"	14.12	4,000
57	18	32,000	"	15.89	4,000
58	19	28,000	"	18.16	4,000
59	20	24,000	"	21.18	4,000
60	21	20,000	493.80†	24.69	None
61	22	20,000	"	24.69	None
62	23	20,000	"	24.69	None
63	24	20,000	"	24.69	None
64*	25	20,000	"	24.69	None
65	26	None*			

* Unless you have decided to convert the remainder as described in text.
† At age 60 waiver of premium no longer effective, premium charge for it no longer payable.

MALE, AGE 41 (FEMALE, AGE 44)
DECREASING TERM TO AGE 65 (24-YEAR DECREASING TERM)

1	2	3	4	5	6
AT YOUR AGE	BEGINNING OF POLICY YEAR	DEATH PROTECTION	ANNUAL PREMIUM	YEARLY COST PER $1,000	YEAR'S DECREASE IN DEATH PROTECTION
41	1	$100,000	$540.40	$ 5.40	$4,200
42	2	95,800	"	5.64	4,200
43	3	91,600	"	5.90	4,200
44	4	87,400	"	6.18	4,200
45	5	83,200	"	6.50	4,200
46	6	79,000	"	6.84	4,200
47	7	74,800	"	7.22	4,200
48	8	70,600	"	7.65	4,200
49	9	66,400	"	8.14	4,200
50	10	62,200	"	8.69	4,300
51	11	57,900	"	9.33	4,200
52	12	53,700	"	10.06	4,200
53	13	49,500	"	10.92	4,200
54	14	45,300	"	11.93	4,200
55	15	41,100	"	13.15	4,200
56	16	36,900	"	14.64	4,200
57	17	32,700	"	16.53	4,200
58	18	28,500	"	18.96	4,200
59	19	24,300	"	22.24	4,300
60	20	20,000	524.20†	26.21	None
61	21	20,000	"	26.21	None
62	22	20,000	"	26.21	None
63	23	20,000	"	26.21	None
64*	24	20,000	"	26.21	None
65	25	None*			

* Unless you have decided to convert the remainder as described in text.
† At age 60 waiver of premium no longer effective, premium charge for it no longer payable.

MALE, AGE 42 (FEMALE, AGE 45)
DECREASING TERM TO AGE 65 (23-YEAR DECREASING TERM)

1	2	3	4	5	6
AT YOUR AGE	BEGINNING OF POLICY YEAR	DEATH PROTECTION	ANNUAL PREMIUM	YEARLY COST PER $1,000	YEAR'S DECREASE IN DEATH PROTECTION
42	1	$100,000	$575.80	$ 5.76	$4,400
43	2	95,600	"	6.02	4,400
44	3	91,200	"	6.31	4,500
45	4	86,700	"	6.64	4,400
46	5	82,300	"	7.00	4,500
47	6	77,800	"	7.40	4,400
48	7	73,400	"	7.84	4,500
49	8	68,900	"	8.36	4,400
50	9	64,500	"	8.93	4,500
51	10	60,000	"	9.60	4,400
52	11	55,600	"	10.36	4,400
53	12	51,200	"	11.25	4,500
54	13	46,700	"	12.33	4,400
55	14	42,300	"	13.61	4,500
56	15	37,800	"	15.23	4,400
57	16	33,400	"	17.24	4,500
58	17	28,900	"	19.92	4,400
59	18	24,500	"	23.50	4,500
60	19	20,000	557.80†	27.89	None
61	20	20,000	"	27.89	None
62	21	20,000	"	27.89	None
63	22	20,000	"	27.89	None
64*	23	20,000	"	27.89	None
65	24	None*			

* Unless you have decided to convert the remainder as described in text.
† At age 60 waiver of premium no longer effective, premium charge for it no longer payable.

MALE, AGE 43 (FEMALE, AGE 46)
DECREASING TERM TO AGE 65 (22-YEAR DECREASING TERM)

1	2	3	4	5	6
AT YOUR AGE	BEGINNING OF POLICY YEAR	DEATH PROTECTION	ANNUAL PREMIUM	YEARLY COST PER $1,000	YEAR'S DECREASE IN DEATH PROTECTION
43	1	$100,000	$613.80	$ 6.14	$4,400
44	2	95,600	"	6.42	4,400
45	3	91,200	"	6.73	4,500
46	4	86,700	"	7.08	4,400
47	5	82,300	"	7.46	4,500
48	6	77,800	"	7.89	4,400
49	7	73,400	"	8.36	4,500
50	8	68,900	"	8.91	4,400
51	9	64,500	"	9.52	4,500
52	10	60,000	"	10.23	4,400
53	11	55,600	"	11.04	4,400
54	12	51,200	"	11.99	4,500
55	13	46,700	"	13.14	4,400
56	14	42,300	"	14.51	4,500
57	15	37,800	"	16.24	4,400
58	16	33,400	"	18.38	4,500
59	17	28,900	"	21.24	4,400
60	18	24,500	594.00†	24.24	4,500
61	19	20,000	"	29.70	None
62	20	20,000	"	29.70	None
63	21	20,000	"	29.70	None
64*	22	20,000	"	29.70	None
65	23	None*			

* Unless you have decided to convert the remainder as described in text.
† At age 60 waiver of premium no longer effective, premium charge for it no longer payable.

MALE, AGE 44 (FEMALE, AGE 47)
DECREASING TERM TO AGE 65 (21-YEAR DECREASING TERM)

1	2	3	4	5	6
AT YOUR AGE	BEGINNING OF POLICY YEAR	DEATH PROTECTION	ANNUAL PREMIUM	YEARLY COST PER $1,000	YEAR'S DECREASE IN DEATH PROTECTION
44	1	$100,000	$654.80	$ 6.55	$4,700
45	2	95,300	"	6.87	4,700
46	3	90,600	"	7.23	4,700
47	4	85,900	"	7.62	4,700
48	5	81,200	"	8.06	4,700
49	6	76,500	"	8.56	4,700
50	7	71,800	"	9.12	4,800
51	8	67,000	"	9.77	4,600
52	9	62,400	"	10.49	4,700
53	10	57,700	"	11.35	4,700
54	11	53,000	"	12.35	4,700
55	12	48,300	"	13.56	4,700
56	13	43,600	"	15.02	4,700
57	14	38,900	"	16.83	4,800
58	15	34,100	"	19.20	4,600
59	16	29,500	"	22.20	4,700
60	17	24,800	632.80†	25.52	4,800
61	18	20,000	"	31.64	None
62	19	20,000	"	31.64	None
63	20	20,000	"	31.64	None
64*	21	20,000	"	31.64	None
65	22	None*			

* Unless you have decided to convert the remainder as described in text.
† At age 60 waiver of premium no longer effective, premium charge for it no longer payable.

MALE, AGE 45 (FEMALE, AGE 48)
25-YEAR DECREASING TERM

1	2	3	4	5	6
AT YOUR AGE	BEGINNING OF POLICY YEAR	DEATH PROTECTION	ANNUAL PREMIUM	YEARLY COST PER $1,000	YEAR'S DECREASE IN DEATH PROTECTION
45	1	$100,000	$807.80	$ 8.08	$4,000
46	2	96,000	"	8.41	4,000
47	3	92,000	"	8.78	4,000
48	4	88,000	"	9.18	4,000
49	5	84,000	"	9.62	4,000
50	6	80,000	"	10.10	4,000
51	7	76,000	"	10.63	4,000
52	8	72,000	"	11.22	4,000
53	9	68,000	"	11.88	4,000
54	10	64,000	"	12.62	4,000
55	11	60,000	"	13.46	4,000
56	12	56,000	"	14.43	4,000
57	13	52,000	"	15.53	4,000
58	14	48,000	"	16.83	4,000
59	15	44,000	"	18.36	4,000
60	16	40,000	776.80†	19.42	4,000
61	17	36,000	"	21.58	4,000
62	18	32,000	"	24.28	4,000
63	19	28,000	"	27.74	4,000
64*	20	24,000	"	32.37	4,000

* Because this is 25-Year Decreasing Term insurance it can be continued as term insurance to age 70 or converted as explained in text.
† At age 60 waiver of premium no longer effective, premium charge for it no longer payable.

MALE, AGE 46 (FEMALE, AGE 49)
25-YEAR DECREASING TERM

1	2	3	4	5	6
AT YOUR AGE	BEGINNING OF POLICY YEAR	DEATH PROTECTION	ANNUAL PREMIUM	YEARLY COST PER $1,000	YEAR'S DECREASE IN DEATH PROTECTION
46	1	$100,000	$890.80	$ 8.91	$4,000
47	2	96,000	"	9.28	4,000
48	3	92,000	"	9.68	4,000
49	4	88,000	"	10.12	4,000
50	5	84,000	"	10.60	4,000
51	6	80,000	"	11.14	4,000
52	7	76,000	"	11.72	4,000
53	8	72,000	"	12.37	4,000
54	9	68,000	"	13.10	4,000
55	10	64,000	"	13.92	4,000
56	11	60,000	"	14.85	4,000
57	12	56,000	"	15.91	4,000
58	13	52,000	"	17.13	4,000
59	14	48,000	"	18.56	4,000
60	15	44,000	855.20†	19.44	4,000
61	16	40,000	"	21.38	4,000
62	17	36,000	"	23.76	4,000
63	18	32,000	"	26.73	4,000
64*	19	28,000	"	30.54	4,000

* Because this is 25-Year Decreasing Term insurance it can be continued as term insurance to age 71 or converted as explained in text.
† At age 60 waiver of premium no longer effective, premium charge for it no longer payable.

MALE, AGE 47 (FEMALE, AGE 50)
25-YEAR DECREASING TERM

1	2	3	4	5	6
AT YOUR AGE	BEGINNING OF POLICY YEAR	DEATH PROTECTION	ANNUAL PREMIUM	YEARLY COST PER $1,000	YEAR'S DECREASE IN DEATH PROTECTION
47	1	$100,000	$981.80	$ 9.82	$4,000
48	2	96,000	"	10.23	4,000
49	3	92,000	"	10.67	4,000
50	4	88,000	"	11.16	4,000
51	5	84,000	"	11.69	4,000
52	6	80,000	"	12.27	4,000
53	7	76,000	"	12.92	4,000
54	8	72,000	"	13.64	4,000
55	9	68,000	"	14.44	4,000
56	10	64,000	"	15.34	4,000
57	11	60,000	"	16.36	4,000
58	12	56,000	"	17.53	4,000
59	13	52,000	"	18.88	4,000
60	14	48,000	940.60†	19.60	4,000
61	15	44,000	"	21.38	4,000
62	16	40,000	"	23.52	4,000
63	17	36,000	"	26.13	4,000
64*	18	32,000	"	29.39	4,000

* Because this is 25-Year Decreasing Term insurance it can be continued as term insurance to age 72 or converted as explained in text.
† At age 60 waiver of premium no longer effective, premium charge for it no longer payable.

MALE, AGE 48 (FEMALE, AGE 51)
25-YEAR DECREASING TERM

1	2	3	4	5	6
AT YOUR AGE	BEGINNING OF POLICY YEAR	DEATH PROTECTION	ANNUAL PREMIUM	YEARLY COST PER $1,000	YEAR'S DECREASE IN DEATH PROTECTION
48	1	$100,000	$1,081.40	$10.81	$4,000
49	2	96,000	"	11.26	4,000
50	3	92,000	"	11.75	4,000
51	4	88,000	"	12.29	4,000
52	5	84,000	"	12.87	4,000
53	6	80,000	"	13.52	4,000
54	7	76,000	"	14.23	4,000
55	8	72,000	"	15.02	4,000
56	9	68,000	"	15.90	4,000
57	10	64,000	"	16.90	4,000
58	11	60,000	"	18.02	4,000
59	12	56,000	"	19.31	4,000
60	13	52,000	1,033.20†	19.87	4,000
61	14	48,000	"	21.53	4,000
62	15	44,000	"	23.48	4,000
63	16	40,000	"	25.83	4,000
64*	17	36,000	"	28.70	4,000

* Because this is 25-Year Decreasing Term insurance it can be continued as term insurance to age 73 or converted as explained in text.
† At age 60 waiver of premium no longer effective, premium charge for it no longer payable.

MALE, AGE 49 (FEMALE, AGE 52)
25-YEAR DECREASING TERM

1	2	3	4	5	6
AT YOUR AGE	BEGINNING OF POLICY YEAR	DEATH PROTECTION	ANNUAL PREMIUM	YEARLY COST PER $1,000	YEAR'S DECREASE IN DEATH PROTECTION
49	1	$100,000	$1,190.00	$11.90	$4,000
50	2	96,000	"	12.40	4,000
51	3	92,000	"	12.93	4,000
52	4	88,000	"	13.52	4,000
53	5	84,000	"	14.17	4,000
54	6	80,000	"	14.88	4,000
55	7	76,000	"	15.66	4,000
56	8	72,000	"	16.53	4,000
57	9	68,000	"	17.50	4,000
58	10	64,000	"	18.59	4,000
59	11	60,000	"	19.83	4,000
60	12	56,000	1,132.80†	20.23	4,000
61	13	52,000	"	21.78	4,000
62	14	48,000	"	23.60	4,000
63	15	44,000	"	25.75	4,000
64*	16	40,000	"	28.32	4,000

* Because this is 25-Year Decreasing Term insurance it can be continued as term insurance to age 74 or converted as explained in text.
† At age 60 waiver of premium no longer effective, premium charge for it no longer payable.

MALE, AGE 50 (FEMALE, AGE 53)
25-YEAR DECREASING TERM

1	2	3	4	5	6
					YEAR'S
	BEGINNING			YEARLY	DECREASE
AT YOUR	OF POLICY	DEATH	ANNUAL	COST PER	IN DEATH
AGE	YEAR	PROTECTION	PREMIUM	$1,000	PROTECTION
50	1	$100,000	$1,308.20	$13.08	$4,000
51	2	96,000	"	13.63	4,000
52	3	92,000	"	14.22	4,000
53	4	88,000	"	14.87	4,000
54	5	84,000	"	15.57	4,000
55	6	80,000	"	16.35	4,000
56	7	76,000	"	17.21	4,000
57	8	72,000	"	18.17	4,000
58	9	68,000	"	19.24	4,000
59	10	64,000	"	20.44	4,000
60	11	60,000	1,239.40†	20.66	4,000
61	12	56,000	"	22.13	4,000
62	13	52,000	"	23.83	4,000
63	14	48.000	"	25.82	4,000
64*	15	44,000	"	28.17	4,000

* Because this is 25-Year Decreasing Term insurance it can be continued as term insurance to age 75 or converted as explained in text.
† At age 60 waiver of premium no longer effective, premium charge for it no longer payable.

MALE, AGE 51 (FEMALE, AGE 54)
20-YEAR DECREASING TERM

1	2	3	4	5	6
					YEAR'S
	BEGINNING			YEARLY	DECREASE
AT YOUR	OF POLICY	DEATH	ANNUAL	COST PER	IN DEATH
AGE	YEAR	PROTECTION	PREMIUM	$1,000	PROTECTION
51	1	$100,000	$1,227.40	$12.27	$5,000
52	2	95,000	"	12.92	5,000
53	3	90,000	"	13.64	5,000
54	4	85,000	"	14.44	5,000
55	5	80,000	"	15.34	5,000
56	6	75,000	"	16.37	5,000
57	7	70,000	"	17.53	5,000
58	8	65,000	"	18.88	5,000
59	9	60,000	"	20.46	5,000
60	10	55,000	1,166.00†	21.20	5,000
61	11	50,000	"	23.32	5,000
62	12	45,000	"	25.91	5,000
63	13	40,000	"	29.15	5,000
64*	14	35,000	"	33.31	5,000

* Because this is 20-Year Decreasing Term insurance it can be continued as term insurance to age 71 or converted as explained in text.
† At age 60 waiver of premium no longer effective, premium charge for it no longer payable.

MALE, AGE 52 (FEMALE, AGE 55)
20-YEAR DECREASING TERM

1	2	3	4	5	6
AT YOUR AGE	BEGINNING OF POLICY YEAR	DEATH PROTECTION	ANNUAL PREMIUM	YEARLY COST PER $1,000	YEAR'S DECREASE IN DEATH PROTECTION
52	1	$100,000	$1,353.00	$13.53	$5,000
53	2	95,000	"	14.24	5,000
54	3	90,000	"	15.03	5,000
55	4	85,000	"	15.92	5,000
56	5	80,000	"	16.91	5,000
57	6	75,000	"	18.04	5,000
58	7	70,000	"	19.33	5,000
59	8	65,000	"	20.82	5,000
60	9	60,000	1,281.60†	21.36	5,000
61	10	55,000	"	23.30	5,000
62	11	50,000	"	25.63	5,000
63	12	45,000	"	28.48	5,000
64*	13	40,000	"	32.04	5,000

* Because this is 20-Year Decreasing Term insurance it can be continued as term insurance to age 72 or converted as explained in text.
† At age 60 waiver of premium no longer effective, premium charge for it no longer payable.

MALE, AGE 53 (FEMALE, AGE 56)
20-YEAR DECREASING TERM

1	2	3	4	5	6
AT YOUR AGE	BEGINNING OF POLICY YEAR	DEATH PROTECTION	ANNUAL PREMIUM	YEARLY COST PER $1,000	YEAR'S DECREASE IN DEATH PROTECTION
53	1	$100,000	$1,491.60	$14.92	$5,000
54	2	95,000	"	15.70	5,000
55	3	90,000	"	16.57	5,000
56	4	85,000	"	17.55	5,000
57	5	80,000	"	18.65	5,000
58	6	75,000	"	19.89	5,000
59	7	70,000	"	21.31	5,000
60	8	65,000	1,407.40†	21.65	5,000
61	9	60,000	"	23.46	5,000
62	10	55,000	"	25.59	5,000
63	11	50,000	"	28.15	5,000
64*	12	45,000	"	31.28	5,000

* Because this is 20-Year Decreasing Term insurance it can be continued as term insurance to age 73 or converted as explained in text.
† At age 60 waiver of premium no longer effective, premium charge for it no longer payable.

MALE, AGE 54 (FEMALE, AGE 57)
20-YEAR DECREASING TERM

1 AT YOUR AGE	2 BEGINNING OF POLICY YEAR	3 DEATH PROTECTION	4 ANNUAL PREMIUM	5 YEARLY COST PER $1,000	6 YEAR'S DECREASE IN DEATH PROTECTION
54	1	$100,000	$1,644.20	$16.44	$5,000
5	2	95,000	"	17.31	5,000
56	3	90,000	"	18.27	5,000
57	4	85,000	"	19.34	5,000
58	5	80,000	"	20.55	5,000
59	6	75,000	"	21.92	5,000
60	7	70,000	1,543.20†	22.05	5,000
61	8	65,000	"	23.74	5,000
62	9	60,000	"	25.72	5,000
63	10	55,000	"	28.06	5,000
64*	11	50,000	"	30.86	5,000

* Because this is 20-Year Decreasing Term insurance it can be continued as term insurance to age 74 or converted as explained in text.
† At age 60 waiver of premium no longer effective, premium charge for it no longer payable.

MALE, AGE 55 (FEMALE, AGE 58)
20-YEAR DECREASING TERM

1 AT YOUR AGE	2 BEGINNING OF POLICY YEAR	3 DEATH PROTECTION	4 ANNUAL PREMIUM	5 YEARLY COST PER $1,000	6 YEAR'S DECREASE IN DEATH PROTECTION
55	1	$100,000	$1,813.60	$18.14	$5,000
56	2	95,000	"	19.09	5,000
57	3	90,000	"	20.15	5,000
58	4	85,000	"	21.34	5,000
59	5	80,000	"	22.67	5,000
60	6	75,000	1,690.00†	22.53	5,000
61	7	70,000	"	24.14	5,000
62	8	65,000	"	26.00	5,000
63	9	60,000	"	28.17	5,000
64*	10	55,000	"	30.73	5,000

* Because this is 20-Year Decreasing Term insurance it can be continued as term insurance to age 75 or converted as explained in text.
† At age 60 waiver of premium no longer effective, premium charge for it no longer payable.

Index